A Dictionary of Medical Management Terms and Initialisms

American College of Physician Executives

Suite 200

4890 West Kennedy Boulevard

Tampa, Florida 33609

813/ 287-2000

ISBN: 0-924674-62-8
Library of Congress Card Number: 97-78155

Printed in the United States of America by Hillsboro Printing Company, Tampa, Florida, United States of America.

Introduction

The American College of Physician Executives took its first step into the world of printed glossaries in 1993, with the introduction of its Glossary of Legal Terms. In subsequent years, we issued glossaries on bioethical terms, health care marketing terms, health insurance terms, managed care terms, medical informatics terms, and medical quality management terms. The final glossary, on financial management terms, was issued in 1995. This dictionary owes much to those earlier efforts, and the College wants to publicly thank Eric Berkowitz, PhD; Mark A. Bloomberg, MD, MBA, FACPE; Charles E. Hollerman, MD, FACPE; Frederick G. Jones, MD, FACPE; Hugh W. Long, MBA, PhD, JD; Edward H. Lowenstein, MD; Sam J.W. Romeo, MD, MBA, FACPE; Todd Sagin, MD, JD; Stephen C. Schoenbaum, MD, MPH, FACPE; and Norman J. Schroeder II, MD, MBA, FACPE for their contributions to the glossaries.

To those earlier volumes, we have added the wealth of terms and definitions that have been captured by the College's Expert System, a computer-based compilation of information on medical management. Finally, we have added initialisms that the physician in management is most likely to encounter. All these materials have been tested by an extraordinary panel of physician leaders. These individuals have tested all our definitions against their very considerable experience and have added terms and definitions that were missed. We would be ungrateful if we did not acknowledge their service on the profession's behalf: Robert Aquino, Nancy Ashbach, Mark Bloomberg, James Casanova, Frederick Gale, Robert Hodge, George Innes, Marianne Kanning, Nicholas Mischler, Toni Mitchell, Robert Pyatt, Sheila Sawyer.

The result, we think, of all these inputs is an excellent guide to the content of medical management and to the terms and concepts that direct it. Most of the terms must be learned and the concepts mastered for success in medical management, so we offer this dictionary as a career management and development tool. As you use it, we hope you will share your impressions with us so that production of future editions can be guided by your experience. Most important, whenever the dictionary fails you, through error or omission, we hope you will call it to our attention so that future editions have greater value.

Finally, a book of this size and complexity requires a staff of individuals to push it through and ensure that it reaches the level of quality imagined by its designers. The College thanks Leslie Burns, Jill Howell, Debi Marsh, Susan Quinn, Remie Cannon Sanz, Carolyn Spinner-Sica, Lou Ellen Williams, and Gwen Wolff for the skills and dedication that they brought to the task of producing the dictionary.

Wesley Curry
Managing Editor, Book Publishing
American College of Physician Executives
Suite 200
4890 W. Kennedy Blvd.
Tampa, FL 33609
813/287-2000
FAX: 813/287-8993
E-Mail: wcurry@acpe.org
January 1998

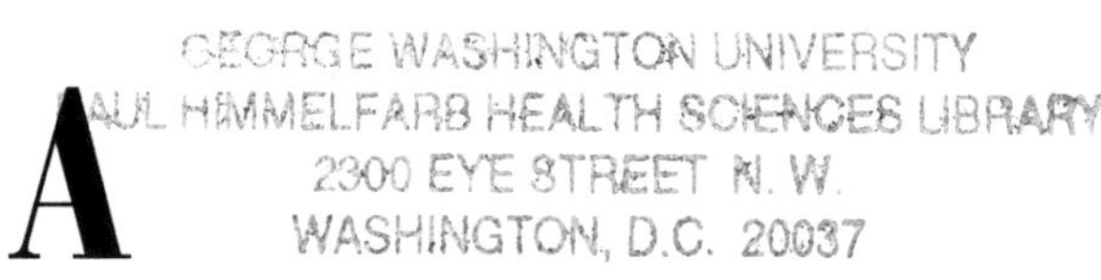

A

AAPCC (Adjusted Average Per Capita Cost): Health Care Financing Administration formula for determining the costs to serve Medicare recipients in a given geographic area.

Abandonment: Improper withdrawal from the care of a patient after the creation of a doctor/patient relationship. Generally, a duty of care continues until the physician's services are no longer required; there is a mutual consent to termination; the patient dismisses the physician; or the physician elects to discontinue care. To avoid abandonment, the physician should provide adequate notice and an adequate opportunity for the patient to obtain substitute care.

ABNA: Achievable benefits not achieved.

Abortifacient: Inducing abortion by artificial means, such as a prescription drug.

Abortion: The forced expulsion of a human fetus from its mother.

Abuse: Improper use or treatment.

Abusus Non Tollit Usum: "Abuse does not take away use." The belief that the potential for abuse is not a sufficient reason for discarding a procedure or treatment.

Academic Health Center: Medical complex consisting of medical school, hospitals, clinics, libraries, administrative facilities, etc.

Acceleration Clause: A clause in any loan agreement or bond indenture that permits the creditor to demand immediate payment of any unpaid principal if other specified terms of the agreement or indenture are violated.

Access: Availability of health care for a predetermined or defined population.

Accident Perils: An underwriting classification used to evaluate the risk of specific occupations.

Accountability: Techniques in accounting that ensure that an organization's assets can be fully identified at all times and that they are used effectively in generating profits.

Accountable Health Plans: Insuring delivery systems that would offer a standardized, federally defined minimum benefit plan to be established by the National Health Board. Proposed as part of the health care reform legislation offered by the Clinton Administration, the concept died in Congress.

Accounting: A system used to identify, measure, and communicate financial information on a business organization. The output of the system is intended to assist organizational managers and outside parties in making informed decisions about the current and historical fiscal performance of the organization.

Accounts Payable: Short-term liabilities representing money owed to creditors, usually suppliers of goods or services to an organization.

Accounts Receivable: Asset representing claims for money owed the organization for the provision of services or the sale of goods.

Accreditation: The process by which an organization or an individual is judged by an agency to meet predetermined standards of performance in the delivery of health care services.

Accrete: To add enrollees to a Medicare managed care health plan.

Accrual Accounting: An accounting method in which revenues are recognized when services are provided or goods are delivered rather than when payment is received. Expenses are recognized, using the "matching principle," when revenue is recognized rather than when a transfer of cash occurs. See *transaction*.

Accrual: Money that is set aside by a managed care plan to cover expenses. The amount is determined by data from the authorization system, the claims system, lag studies, and the plan's history.

Accrued: A revenue or expense that has been recognized even though the related payment has not been made. See *transaction*.

ACHE: American College of Healthcare Executives.

Achievable Benefits Not Achieved (ABNA): The list of operational targets for any quality improvement program or system. Essentially, ABNA are the areas of possible improvement.

Acid Test Ratio: A financial ratio defined as current assets divided by current liabilities. Also called "quick ratio."

ACLM: American College of Legal Medicine.

ACME: American Council on Medical Education.

ACOHA: American College of Osteopathic Hospital Administrators.

Acquisition Cost: All costs (price, legal fees, transportation charges, installation costs, and the like) required to purchase and install an asset.

ACPE: American College of Physician Executives.

ACR (Average Cost Rate): The premium charged by a plan to provide Medicare benefits to a group account, adjusted for the greater intensity and frequency of Medicare services.

Action in Personam: A lawsuit against a person on the basis of personal liability.

Action in Rem: A lawsuit to determine title to property.

Action: Lawsuit; the legal demand for one's rights asserted in a court. If something is "actionable," it provides legal ground for a complaint in court.

Active Storage: Auxiliary memory dedicated to data that have long-term value and must be accessed easily and quickly. Commonly found on floppy or hard disks.

Activities of Daily Living: Eating, clothing oneself, ambulation, and all the other basic functions of life. Used as a base determination of the quality of a person's life.

Activity Ratio: Any financial ratio that relates a stock or fixed quantity at a point in time to a flow or quantity of activity during a period of time. For example, a ratio in which the numerator comes from an end-of-period balance sheet and the denominator comes from the income statement for that period.

Activity-Based Cost System: Cost accounting based on the costs of individual activities involved in the design, production, and distribution of a good or service. Used to assign overhead costs or expenses to specific activities.

Activity-by-Case Analysis: Ranking of payers in order of their activity during a specific period.

Actuarial Assumptions: Assumptions used by an actuary in the determination of expected costs and revenues. Examples of areas in which such assumptions are made include utilization rates and age and gender mix of enrollees.

Actuarial Valuation Method: The actuarial value is the value of each option with all employees participating in that option. A value is set on the basis of the amount of cost-sharing that is required. This method results in less rate volatility.

Actuary: An insurance expert who applies mathematical probability theory to the calculation of premiums and other values for risk-based goods, such as insurance policies, annuities, and capitated health plans.

Acuity Index Method (AIM): One of several commercially available systems for adjusting utilization, outcome, and other medical quality management data for severity of illness. A registered trademark of Iameter, Inc.

Acute Physiology and Chronic Health Evaluation (APACHE): One of several commercially available systems for adjusting utilization, outcome, and other medical quality management data for severity of illness. A registered trademark of APACHE Medical Systems, Inc.

Ad Damnum Clause: The clause in the plaintiff's pleading that states the damages claimed.

Ad Litem: Latin phrase—"for purposes of the suit" being prosecuted. Frequently used as guardian ad litem—a person appointed to prosecute or defend a suit on behalf of an incapacitated party.

Adam Smith: Scottish economist of the 18th Century who wrote *The Wealth of Nations*.

Address: The computer designation for a particular cell of memory and its contents.

Adequate Disclosure: Inclusion of all material items in financial statements.

Adjective Law: Rules of legal practice that set forth methods of enforcing rights created by substantive law. For example, service of process (communication of court papers to the defendant) is a matter of adjective law.

Adjudication: Processing of a claim to determine proper payment.

Adjusted Average Per Capita Cost (AAPCC): The Health Care Financing Administration's estimate of how much it costs to provide care for Medicare patients under fee-for-service conditions in a particular area. The estimate comprises 122 rate cells, 120 of which are factored for age, gender, eligibility, institutional status, and whether patients are eligible for both Part A and Part B of Medicare. The remaining cells are for patients with end-stage renal disease.

Adjusted Community Rate: Factor used by HMOs and CMPs with Medicare risk contracts to decide what premium should be charged for providing the exact Medicare-covered benefits to a group account adjusted to allow for more utilization by Medicare recipients.

ADL: Activities of daily living.

Administered Vertical Marketing System: A system in which one member is formally or informally designated as "captain" and dictates actions or policies within the channel for particular products or services.

Administrative Agency: A government body charged with administering or implementing particular legislation.

Administrative Cost or Expense: A cost or an expense related to the organization as a whole rather than to a specific good or service or to a specific function or activity of the organization.

Administrative Costs: All expenses associated with nonclinical aspects of health care delivery by a managed care plan.

Administrative Fee: A specific contractual charge for the costs of nonclinical services in the provision of health care.

Administrative Loading: See *loading*.

Administrative Services Only (ASO): A self-insurance arrangement in which an organization contracts with an outside firm for administration of an employer's health insurance program for employees but under which the employer retains responsibility for payment of claims. See *self-insured group* and *third-party administrator*.

Admission: A statistical term used to measure hospital utilization. An admission is the entry of a patient into a hospital as an inpatient, without regard for the length of the patient's stay.

Adoption Curve: A graphical depiction of how and when different groups accept new ideas.

Adoption process: The steps individuals go through on the way to accepting or rejecting a new idea.

ADP: Automatic data processing.

Advance Directive: A mechanism by which patients can make their wishes for medical treatment known for the time when they may be unable to communicate their wishes or may lack decision-making capacity. It is the umbrella term under which are found living wills, power of attorney, informed consent, and other aspects of an individual's wishes for medical treatment in a life-or-death situation.

Adverse Event: The occurrence during a patient's encounter with the health care system of a single unanticipated experience, such as falling out of a hospital bed or suffering a drug reaction, that may lead to an adverse outcome. Adverse events may or may not be the result of negligence.

Adverse Outcome: The negative impact on a patient's health status that results from an adverse event or series of adverse events. More generally, any unanticipated, negative result for a specific patient in the provision of health care services.

Adverse Selection: Design of insurance programs so as to discourage coverage for persons who are more likely to make claims. From the insurer's point of view, the greater tendency of persons who are more likely to make claims to apply for or continue insurance policies.

Advertising Agencies: Firms of specialists in planning and handling mass selling details for advertisers.

Advertising Allowances: Price reductions offered to firms in the channel of distribution to encourage them to advertise or otherwise promote a supplier's products or services.

Advertising Campaign: A set of messages with a single theme that is repeatedly conveyed to the target audience over an extended period.

Advertising Platform: The specific issues and product benefits that a marketer wishes to convey in an advertising message.

Advertising Theme: The parts of an advertising message that are repeated throughout the campaign.

Advertising: Any paid form of nonpersonal presentation of ideas, goods, or services by an identified sponsor. Some approaches used in health care include direct mailings to former patients or residents of the market area and publishing annual reports and hospital newspapers.

Affective Component (of an attitude): The emotional feeling of favorableness or unfavorableness that results from a person's evaluation of an object.

Affidavit: A voluntary statement of facts, or a voluntary declaration in writing of facts, that a person swears to be true before an official authorized to administer an oath.

Affiliation: A form of joint venture or cooperation in which competitors or others coordinate and integrate their activities without completely merging or consolidating. Process by which an organization becomes part of another organization but retains its legally separate status.

Affinity Diagram: A tool for organizing large volumes of ideas or issues into major groupings. Major themes emerge from the diagram to clarify a disorganized picture. This tool is useful at the start of a project to help focus on major issues and real problems.

Affinity Group: The members of a formal professional association or other organization whose members are united on the basis of common goals or interests—e.g., accountants, lawyers, physicians, Harvard University graduates, etc.

Affirmative Defense: A response to allegations in a complaint that constitutes a defense even if the allegations being pressed are true. In effect, an affirmative defense avoids all or part of the liability by presenting new evidence to avoid judgment, rather than by denying the facts alleged in the complaint. Common examples include the statute of limitations and the contributory negligence of the opposing party.

Aftercare: Services that are provided to patients after hospitalization.

Age of Accounts: The time elapsed since an existing accounts payable or accounts receivable was recognized in accounting.

Age-Adjusted Rates: Setting rates on the basis of the age of the insured population. For example, the elderly are more likely to require expensive medical care and younger people are much less likely to do so. To make health care affordable for everyone, the rate would be set high enough to accommodate the sicker population but low enough to be affordable to all.

Agency for Health Care Policy and Research (AHCPR): Created by the Omnibus Budget Reconciliation Act (OBRA) of 1989, this federal agency is housed within the Public Health Service of the Department of Health and Human Services. AHCPR is charged with funding and coordinating a national health research effort aimed at medical treatment effectiveness and clinical outcomes.

The agency is also charged with developing or fostering the development of clinical guidelines and criteria for measurement of care related to guidelines.

Agency Relationship: A relationship in which one party is legally authorized to perform acts for or on behalf of another party.

Agency: A relationship whereby one entrusts the performance of an act to another who assumes the duty to so act. It is often characterized by the existence of a right of the principal or master to exercise control over the agent or servant. Such a relationship may be by agreement of the parties or may be implied by law to exist under the circumstances. See *apparent agency.*

Agenda for Change: A major initiative of the Joint Commission on Accreditation of Healthcare Organizations that shifts the emphasis in the hospital accreditation process from facilities and programs to patient outcomes.

Age-Sex Rating: A method for structuring capitation payments on the basis of enrollee/membership age and gender.

Aggregate Claims: The aggregate claims expected under a policy are a primary element in the calculation of premium rates. The factor is determined by multiplying the claim frequency rate by the average amount of claims and then multiplying the result by the number of insureds.

AGPA: American Group Practice Association (now the American Medical Group Association).

AHA: American Hospital Association.

AHC: Academic health center.

AHCA: American Health Care Association.

AHCPR: Agency for Health Care Policy and Research.

AHDMS: Automated hospital data management system.

AHEC: Area health education center.

AHIS: Automated hospital information system.

AHPA: American Health Planning Association.

AI: Artificial intelligence.

AIDSLINE: On-line MEDLARS database on AIDS.

AIDSTRIALS: On-line MEDLARS database on AIDS drugs.

AIDA Model: The belief that marketing of a service or product requires four promotional jobs—to get attention, to hold interest, to arouse desire, and to obtain action.

AIM: See *Acuity Index Method*.

Aleatory Contract: A contract under which one party agrees to provide something of value to another party if a specified event occurs.

Algorithm: A linked series of "if...then" statements. A convenient format for expressing a clinical practice guideline and its branched logic. Often presented as a flow chart.

All-Payer Program: A health care reimbursement program under which prices are set equally among all payers to distribute the bad debt burden.

Allegations: The position of a party to a lawsuit, stated in the pleadings.

Alliance: A group of health care organizations that maintain separate legal and organizational status but join for administrative and functional purposes.

Allied Health Care: Services such as mental health, podiatry, and chiropractic.

Allied Health Personnel: Licensed health care workers other than physicians, dentists, optometrists, chiropractors, podiatrists, and nurses.

Allocation (Allocating): The process of spreading a dollar amount such as a cost, an expense, or revenue from one to two or more accounts, goods, activities, or periods.

All-or-Nothing Constraint: A condition of membership in a managed care plan under which members must receive all health care services through the plan or they receive no reimbursement.

Allowable Charges: The amount that a medical plan can charge for services, based on fee schedules or negotiated rates.

Allowable Costs: See *allowed amounts*.

Allowance: The difference between an amount charged and the amount actually received for providing a service. Examples of allowances are a charity allowance (difference between charges and amounts received from or on behalf of indigent patients, even if the latter amount is zero), courtesy allowance or policy discount (difference between charges and amounts received from physicians and other health professionals, "accept assignment patients," clergy, employees, and employees' dependents), contractual adjustments (difference between charges and amounts received from third-party payers under contracts), and bad debt allowance (estimates of what cannot be collected, even after best good faith efforts to do so). The terms "deduction" and "provision" are sometimes used as synonyms.

Allowance for Bad Debts (or Allowance for Uncollectibles): An adjustment to accounts receivable based on an estimate of uncollectible accounts. The revenue reduction is recognized at the time the allowance is entered, so that the later actual write-off of specific accounts receivable has no effect on revenues or expenses at that time.

Allowed (Allowable) Amounts: Under retrospective payment, the portions of a provider's expenses that will be reimbursed after the elimination of all expenses that are "not medically necessary."

All-Patient Diagnosis-Related Groups: System used in New York since 1987 for prospective payment for all non-Medicare inpatient services, taking into account cost variance among age groups and patient types. DRGs can be primary or secondary, and there is a classification for outliers. Massachusetts, Maine, and Washington also use some form of AP-DRGs for payment or budget reconciliation.

All-Payer Contract: An arrangement under which payment for delivery of health services is made regardless of the type of health care product or of the revenue source.

All-Payer System: A health plan with uniform prices for all payers.

ALOS: Average length of stay.

Alternate Care: Care provided in lieu of hospitalization or by nontraditional providers, such as midwives.

Alternative Delivery System: General term for delivery and financing mechanisms other than traditional fee-for-service and indemnity. Includes prepaid health plans, HMOs, PPOs, and primary care case management programs.

Alternative Minimum Tax: A method of calculating income taxes that limits the use of deductions and tax credits, thereby increasing tax liability.

Alternative Reproduction: Technologies, such as artificial insemination, that promote conception and pregnancy.

Altruism: Unselfish regard for the welfare of others.

Ambulatory Care: Health care services provided to patients on an ambulatory basis, rather than by admission to a hospital or other health care facility. The services may be a part of a hospital, augmenting its inpatient services, or may be provided at a freestanding facility.

Ambulatory Care Facilities: Facilities that administer health services to individuals who do not require hospitalization or institutionalization.

Ambulatory Care Review: A form of utilization review that allows quantification of the extent of health care services provided in an outpatient setting.

Ambulatory Case Mix System: A system that provides severity adjustment for outpatient services.

Ambulatory Patient Groups (APGs): A system for classifying ambulatory patients having similar demographic, diagnostic, and/or treatment characteristics into groups within which each patient is expected to have relatively homogeneous use of resources for treatment. Groups are established for the purpose of generating a rate or fee schedule comprising a single payment for each group independent of actual resource use by each patient in the group.

Ambulatory Visit Groups (AVGs): A case-based reimbursement system that shifts more risk to the physician. Similar to incentive arrangements.

Amenities: The nonclinical aspects of a patient's encounter with the health care delivery system, such as food service, waiting room decor, parking convenience, and the like, that have a substantial bearing on the patient's judgment of health care quality.

American Association of Foundations for Medical Care: Former trade association for HMOs, now called the American Managed Care and Review Association.

American Managed Care and Review Association: A trade association representing managed indemnity plans, PPOs, MCOs, and HMOs.

American National Standard Code Information Exchange (ASCII): A seven-bit code for the exchange of alphanumeric data among data processing and data communication equipment. May be referred to as "unformatted." (See EBCDIC.)

AMHT: Automated multiphasic health testing.

AMIA: American Medical Informatics Association.

Amniocentesis: Prenatal diagnostic technique in which a needle is inserted through a pregnant woman's abdominal and uterine walls to withdraw fluid from the amniotic sac containing fetal amniocytes. Sometimes performed to determine fetal sex or chromosomal abnormality.

Amortization: Any of several methods for recognizing the acquisition costs of assets or the terminal costs of satisfying liabilities as expenses at the time of benefit or use. The process is called depreciation for plant and equipment, depletion for natural resources, and amortization for intangibles. See *depreciation*; also see *intangible assets*.

AMRS: Automated medical record system.

Analog Data: Presentation of information exactly as it originally occurs or is measured. For instance, a telephone transmission is an analog presentation of the original voice data. See *digital data*.

Analog-to-Digital Conversion: A process or device by which analog data are translated into digital form.

Ancillary Services: Radiological, laboratory, outpatient diagnostic, and other medical services provided in an adjunct role for a procedure or treatment.

Animal Experimentation: Conducting experiments on animals to advance medicine and science by finding cures for diseases or new methods of treatment.

Anniversary: The beginning date of a managed care contract, at which time a health plan member may elect to continue or terminate health plan coverage.

Annual Claim Costs: The expected number of claims for a year multiplied by the average amount paid for a claim. May be calculated by age, gender, occupation, and geographical region.

Annuity: A series of payments at regular intervals.

Annuity Factor: The factor that, when multiplied by the first cash flow of an annuity, generates a good that is the present value of the entire remaining annuity.

Answer: A document filed with the court that contains the response of the defendant to the allegations set out in the plaintiff's complaint.

Antiselection: See *adverse selection*.

Antitrust: Any of a variety of state and federal laws that proscribe organizational activity that is anticompetitive in nature.

Antitrust Immunity: The specific legislative or judicial exclusion of an entity from the restrictions of antitrust law. The Health Care Quality Improvement Act of 1986, for example, provides protection from antitrust litigation for those legitimately involved in the peer review process.

Antitrust Injury: Injury resulting directly from a lessening of competition, not merely from harm to an individual competitor.

Antitrust Laws: Those federal and state laws, and their enforcement, that protect trade and commerce from unlawful restraints and monopolies or unfair business practices.

AOHA: American Osteopathic Hospital Association.

APACHE: See Acute Physiology and Chronic Health Evaluation.

APGs: See *ambulatory patient groups*.

APHA: American Protestant Hospital Association, American Public Health Association.

APhA: American Pharmaceutical Association.

Apparent Agency: An agency relationship created not by agreement, but rather due to circumstances created by the parties that indicate that an agency existed. Observers would assume that one party was acting as agent for another. For example, an emergency department physician has, under certain circumstances, been held to be the apparent agent of a hospital even though he or she was not, in fact, employed by the hospital.

Apparent Authority: The power of an agent to bind an organization to third-party contracts based on the agent's acts or omissions rather than on an express authorization by the organization.

Appellant: The party who takes an appeal from one court or jurisdiction to a different one. The party who appeals the decision of a lower court and brings it to a court of higher jurisdiction.

Appellate Court: A court to which the judgment reached in a trial court is appealed.

Appellee: The party in a case against whom an appeal is lodged. Another name for the appellee is the respondent, i.e., the party who does not want the appeal to successfully overturn the lower court ruling.

Applicant: The party applying for an insurance policy.

Application Program: Instructions to the computer for handling specific user projects or applications, such as accounting, word processing, inventory control, medical records, and the like.

Application: The form completed by an applicant to provide information to the insurance company to guide it in its decision to accept or reject the risk.

Apportionment of Damages: The proration of an award determined by verdict among those entitled to receive its benefit or against those obligated to pay.

Apportionment of Fault: The proration of responsibility for damages among those whose acts contributed to the injuries or loss. For example, a plaintiff may be partially responsible for his or her own injury or loss and may be apportioned a percentage of fault that may reduce or bar his or her recovery. Additionally, where multiple defendants have contributed to an injury or loss, they may each be assigned a percentage of fault. Depending on the rules of that jurisdiction, such an apportionment may form the basis for determining the amount of the total verdict for which each party is responsible.

Appreciation: An increase in the economic worth of an asset.

Appropriateness: The degree to which a medical intervention meets existing standards of care for the specific medical condition it addresses, as well as standards of effectiveness and efficiency, within the immediate geographic community. Appropriate care is that for which the benefits are known or believed to exceed the risks.

Appropriateness of Care: Determination that treatment or procedures are medically necessary and tailored to patients' needs.

Appropriation: In government, the authorization of a specific amount of funding for a specific purpose over a specified time.

Arbitrage: The simultaneous purchase in one market and sale in another market of an identical (pure arbitrage) or similar (risk arbitrage) security or commodity in order to make a profit on market price differences.

Arbitration: The submission of stalled negotiations to a third party for decision making.

Architecture: The design of a computer's internal operations—directories, memory, programs, input/output structure, etc. Also, the design of the computer with regard to all peripheral devices—printers, modems, etc.

Archival Storage: Use of hard disk and magnetic tape for the retention of information for long-term use. Commonly used for back-up, documentary, and legal data.

Aretaic Ethics: Placing primary emphasis on the character of moral agents instead of on the ends of action or on the rules or principles of ethics.

ARNP: Advanced registered nurse practitioner.

Artificial Insemination: Implantation of semen from a man into a woman's genital tract.

Artificial Intelligence (AI): Simulation by computers of human reasoning and learning functions.

ASCII: American Standard Code for Information Exchange.

Assembler: A program that translates assembly-language programs into machine-language programs.

Assembly Language: Low-level mnemonic instructions for communication with computers.

Asset Purchase: The acquisition of resources expected to produce future financial benefit.

Asset Turnover: A financial ratio of net sales or revenues divided by the average value of assets during the period in which the sales were made or the revenue was generated. It purports to be a measure of the effectiveness of asset use.

Asset: The future financial benefit or service potential associated with an accounting transaction. An asset may be tangible (fixed) or intangible and short-term or long-term.

Assets Limited as to Use: Assets, the use of which has been restricted by discretionary choice of the organization's governing board either on its own initiative or by agreement with an outside party. See *restricted assets*.

Assignable: The extent to which something of value owed to party A by party B (obligation X) can be used to satisfy obligation Y of party A to party C by authorizing party B to deliver the satisfaction of obligation X directly to party C. For example, a patient (party A) who owes money (obligation Y) to a provider (party C) for care delivered to party A has a claim (obligation X) for that care on an insurance company (party B). Party A's claim on party B (obligation X) is readily assignable to party C in total or partial fulfillment of obligation Y, what the patient owes the provider.

Assignment of Benefits: Payment directly to a provider of care. Usually necessitates a contract between the health plan and the provider or written permission from the subscriber.

Assignment, Accepting: Agreement by the provider to accept payment from the third-party payer and not to seek payment, other than copayments and deductibles, from the patient.

Assorting: Putting together a variety of products to give a target market what it wants.

Assumption of Risk: The plaintiff's consent to accept a risk that he or she has reason to anticipate. An express assumption of risk arises where the plaintiff specifically agrees in advance to accept a particular risk resulting from the defendant's negligence. An express agreement to assume a risk must not violate public policy, and the language must be clear and unambiguous. An implied assumption of risk exists where the plaintiff does not expressly assume the risk but, nevertheless, knowingly and willingly encounters the risk. While the plaintiff-patient can assume the risk of untoward consequences resulting from the nonnegligent treatment of an ailment, the plaintiff cannot ordinarily assume the consequences of the physician's negligent conduct.

Attempt to Monopolize: Conduct short of actual monopolization that is prohibited by Section 2 of the Sherman Act. There are two elements to an attempt to monopolize claim: (1) specific intent to destroy competition or build monopoly and (2) a dangerous probability that the attempt will be successful in the relevant market.

Attending Physician's Statement (APS): A form completed by a physician who has treated an insured or potential insured for an illness or injury that contains information used in deciding to cover the risk or to settle a claim.

Attestation: Affirmation of a fact, or to bear witness.

Attitude: A person's point of view toward something. In a health care organization, attitudes regarding the organization and its exchanges are critical. It is common practice to monitor the attitudes of active constituents, such as medical staffs, professional employees, and patients.

Attribute Data: Classification or accounting of events, items, or units on the basis of their quality characteristics. Data are usually expressed as whole numbers on a discrete scale of measurement.

Attribution Rules: The treatment (for tax and regulatory purposes) of securities owned by relatives and affiliates of a taxpayer as if they were owned by the taxpayer.

Attrition Rate: Disenrollment as a percentage of total membership.

Audit Committee: A committee of a governing board that nominates external auditors and oversees their work.

Audit: Systematic inspection of accounting records in accordance with generally accepted auditing standards.

Audit Trail: References in accounting entries or postings to the underlying information sources.

Auditor: A person or organization that checks the accuracy, fairness, and acceptability of accounting records and statements.

Auditor's Report: The auditor's statement of (1) the work done in the auditing process and (2) the resulting opinion on the financial statements. An opinion that the statements are in compliance with Generally Accepted Accounting Principles (GAAP) without exception is called a "clean opinion."

Augmented Product: A product that has been enhanced by a set of benefits that consumers do not expect or that exceed their expectations.

AUPHA: Association of University Programs in Health Administration.

Authoritarianism: Seeking weakness in others, then setting out to control and manipulate. Favoring absolute obedience to authority, as opposed to individual freedom.

Authorization: Approval by a health plan or insurer of care for a patient. See *preauthorization*.

Automated Patient Record: Immediate placement of medical record information into computer form. In purest form, eliminates need for paper record altogether. Provides for retrieval of data from multiple locations and ability to extract data for quality indicators.

Automatic Binding Limit: The limit on the amount of reinsurance that a reinsurer will provide.

Automatic Reinsurance Treaty: An agreement by a reinsurer to automatically provide reinsurance in excess of the retention limit up to the automatic binding limit.

Automatic Stay: A petition filed under bankruptcy law. It prevents creditors from collecting pre-petition debt.

Autonomy: Self-governance. As an ethical principle, autonomy is defined as a guide to respecting others as autonomous and enhancing, supporting, or restoring autonomy. See *Informed Consent*.

Auxiliary Memory: Hard disks, floppy disks, and magnetic tape storage of information or programs not needed in main memory.

Availability: The degree to which an appropriate intervention or care is available to meet the needs of patients.

Average Collection Period: The ratio given by accounts receivable at a particular time divided by the average daily revenues for a defined period.

Average Cost Per Unit: The total cost of producing a product or service divided by the related quantity of the product or service.

Average Cost: The sum of money paid or the amount of a liability incurred to purchase assets, or the aggregate cost of producing assets, divided by the number of units purchased or produced, respectively.

Average Daily Census: The sum of the number of patients served each day in a given period divided by the number of days in the period.

Average Fixed Cost Per Unit: The total fixed cost of producing a product or service divided by the related quantity of the product or service.

Average Length of Stay: The sum of the patient days in a given period divided by the total number of patients served.

Average Payment Rate (APR): The money that the Health Care Financing Administration could pay an HMO or CMP for services to Medicare recipients under a risk contract. The figure is determined by the average per capita cost for the service area adjusted for expected enrollment characteristics. The payment to the plan cannot be higher than the average cost rate, but it can be less.

Average Variable Cost Per Unit: The total variable cost of producing a product or service divided by the related quantity of the product or service.

Average-Cost Pricing: Determining the market price of a product or service by adding a reasonable markup to its average cost.

Avoidable Cost: An incremental or variable cost, sometimes called an out-of-pocket cost.

B

Back-Date: To make the date of a policy earlier than the date of the application.

Bad Apple Theory: The quality assurance principle that medical quality can be improved by identifying providers who are most at negative variance from measured averages in the provision of care and working to adjust their behavior back to norms.

Bad Debt: An account that is written off the books because of the expectation that the debtor will not pay; uncollectible accounts receivable. See *allowance for bad debts.*

Bait Pricing: Setting low prices to attract customers but then trying to sell more expensive models or brands once the customer is in the store.

Balance Billing: A provider's billing a patient for charges not paid by the insurance plan, even if the charges are higher than the plan's allowable payment or are considered medically unnecessary. Managed care and service plans often prohibit balance billing except for copayments, coinsurance, and deductibles.

Balance Sheet: A financial accounting statement that shows the assets, liabilities, and owners' equity or net worth of an entity. It is sometimes called a "statement of financial position."

Balloon Payment: The final payment on a loan, consisting of all unpaid principal, typically most or all of the amount borrowed, and any remaining accumulated interest.

BAMM: British Association of Medical Managers.

Bandwidth: In the transmission of information, the amount of data in bits that can be transmitted per unit of time.

Bankruptcy: Legal status of an insolvent entity (one in which liabilities exceed assets). To achieve bankrupt status, the entity must file a legal petition that must be accepted by the courts under state or federal bankruptcy law.

Bargaining Contract: A contract under which all parties set its terms and conditions.

Barrier to Entry: A condition, usually financial in nature, that makes it difficult for new producers or sellers to enter a market.

Baseband: Transmission of information in which a single, unmodulated stream of data is involved.

Basic Health Services: Services that all federally qualified HMOs must offer.

Basic List Price: The price that final customers or users are normally asked to pay for a product or service.

Basic Sales Tasks: Order getting, order taking, and customer supporting.

Basis: The ascribing of an acquisition cost or value to an asset at the time of its sale in order to compute the overall gain or loss to the asset holder.

Batch Mode: Control of computer usage by a central staff, to which users send projects and then wait for results. The process may involve remote transmission, whereby projects are transmitted by modem to the central point.

Batch Program: Method of processing of groups of data that have been collected over time or that must be accounted for periodically.

Battery: Nonconsensual touching. For example, a battery occurs where, absent an emergency or other legally justifiable reason, a patient is treated without consent.

Battle of the Brands: Competition between dealer brands and manufacturer brands.

Baud Rate: The speed at which data are transmitted, expressed in bits per second.

BCA: Blue Cross Association.

BC/BS: Blue Cross Blue Shield plan.

BCD: Binary coded decimal.

Bed Leasing: A reimbursement method in which a set number of beds are leased from a hospital for a set sum. Even if the beds aren't used, the plan has access to them if needed.

Behavior: The manner in which individuals conduct themselves in response to environmental stimulation.

Behavioral Health Care: Systems or processes of diagnosis and treatment for mental health or substance abuse disorders.

Behavior Modification: The use of medications and psychological and environmental manipulations to modify individuals' behavior. Usually refers to methods to diminish maladaptive and socially unacceptable behavior.

Belief: A person's opinion about something.

Benchmark: The overall performance or the performance in a specific case of an organization or individual that is judged to represent the best achievable standard for a product or service.

Benchmarking: A comparison of provider performance with other providers (external benchmarking) or against the provider's own performance (internal benchmarking).

Beneficence: An act intended to further the well-being of others, a principle that underlies the goals of most social and health care organizations. See *paternalism*.

Beneficiary: The person or entity entitled to benefits under a policy.

Beneficiary Protection: Methods for protecting consumers from fraudulent plan practices.

Benefit Design: The process by which services to be covered in a health plan are selected.

Benefit Differentials: Increased sums a plan pays when a subscriber receives services from a preferred provider.

Benefit Level: The extent to which the costs of a particular service are reimbursed.

Benefit Package: The specific services covered under a plan or policy.

Benefit Year: The calendar year during which benefits are in effect.

Benefit-Cost Approach: See *cost-benefit approach*.

Benefit-Risk Approach: See *risk-benefit approach*.

Best Alternative to a Negotiated Agreement (BATNA): Addresses what an organization's options are if an agreement is not reached.

Best Interests Standard: Legal standard that focuses on physical and financial risks, harms, and benefits to ensure that the best interests of the parties to the legal issue are served.

Bid Pricing: Offering a specific price for each possible sale rather than setting a price that applies for all customers.

Bilateral Contract: A contract under which both parties can be forced to perform as promised.

Bill Audit: Any method of checking the accuracy of bills.

Binding Arbitration: Use of an outside professional to resolve disputes among providers, patients, and the plan. When the professional's help is enlisted, the parties agree to accept any decision reached.

Binding Receipt: A premium receipt that makes insurance coverage available until the insurance company rejects the application or issues a policy. See *temporary insurance agreement*.

Bioethics: Methods and principles for dealing with ethical problems and decisions arising in the delivery of medical care and in medical research.

Biotechnology: An applied biological science, such as bioengineering, or its products, such as recombinant DNA technology.

Birth Control: Artificial measures taken to prevent conception.

Bit Map: The digital representation of an image or a graphic in memory. The memory bits have a one-on-one correspondence with the image or graphic pixels on the monitor screen.

Bit: An electronic switch in computer memory that assumes a value of 0 or 1 (off or on). All alphanumeric data in computer memory are constructed from bits and bytes.

Blended Rates: Rates based partly on manually rated data and partly on experience-rated data that are used to determine the premium for a group.

Blood Usage Review: Monitoring of surgical notes and medical records to ensure optimum use of blood products in surgical procedures.

BLS: Bureau of Labor Statistics.

Blue Cross Plan: One of several regional not-for-profit health insurance companies, affiliated through the national Blue Cross Blue Shield Association, that provide a wide range of health insurance products. Originally founded for coverage of hospital health care expenses, the plans now are frequently joined with Blue Shield Plans and offer both indemnity and prepaid coverage.

Blue Shield Plan: One of several regional not-for-profit health insurance plans that offer policies for coverage of physician services.

Body Systems Count: A proprietary severity-of-illness indexing system offered by the Commission on Professional and Hospital Activities, Ann Arbor, Mich.

Bona Fide: Genuine. An agreement made in good faith.

Bond: A legal certificate held as evidence of debt. The bond, in addition to identifying the debtor, specifies the amount of the debt, the interest rate, and terms of repayment.

Bond Indenture: The contract between bondholders and the bond issuers. It includes all of the items specified on the face of the bond, plus put or call provisions and all covenants.

Bond Ratings: Categorizations of bonds according to their risk characteristics. The categories typically are given alphabetic labels (e.g., AAA, Baa) by the independent firms that assign such ratings. See *credit rating*.

Book Value: The amount shown in an organization's financial books for any asset, liability, or owners' equity item.

Boot: Cash or property received in exchange for a capital asset that does not qualify as like-kind property. Also, to start a computer so that its operational programs are loaded and available for use.

Booting: See *bootstrap*.

Bootstrap: A set of instructions that is permanently installed in the computer's read only memory and that is used each time the computer is turned on. Execution of the bootstrap is called booting the computer.

Borrowed Servant Doctrine: A legal status that results when an employer loans an employee to another company. It generally requires that the employee come under the direct supervision and control of the party to whom he or she is loaned. In certain jurisdictions, this doctrine results in the shifting of responsibility for the acts of the servant to the individual who borrows the servant (under the doctrine of respondeat superior). For example, a nurse employed by a hospital could, under certain circumstances, become the borrowed servant to a staff physician (e.g., a nurse working under a surgeon in the OR).

Boycott: Concerted action by two or more competing persons or distinct business entities to prevent another competitor from having access to a particular service, product, facility, or market such that there is an anticompetitive effect.

BPS: Bits per second.

Brain Death: Irreversible cerebral damage as indicated by a flat electroencephalogram reading. See *Harvard Test*.

Brainstorming: A method of generating new ideas that consists of holding group discussions in which a specific problem or goal is set and no suggested solution is criticized.

Brand Equity: The monetary value attached to a brand's overall strength in the market.

Brand Extension: The practice of giving a new product category the brand name of an existing category.

Brand Familiarity: The degree to which customers recognize and accept a company's brand.

Brand Insistence: Insistence by customers on having a firm's branded product or service and the willingness to search for it.

Brand Name: A name, term, symbol, or design—or a combination—used to identify a product or service.

Brand Preference: The tendency of target customers to usually choose one brand over other brands, perhaps because of habit or favorable past experience.

Brand Recognition: The degree to which customers remember the brand of a product or service.

Brand Rejection: The tendency of the potential customer not to buy a brand, unless its image is changed.

Break-Even Analysis: A process to determine whether a firm will be able to cover all its costs at a particular price for its product or service.

Break-Even Point (BEP): That level of sales, in either units or dollars, of a good or service at which its total revenues and total direct costs are exactly equal. See *cost-profit-volume analysis.*

Breakthrough Opportunities: Market conditions that help a firm develop hard-to-copy marketing strategies that will be profitable for a long time.

Broadband: Transmission of information in which data signals are modulated within a frequency range and several signals can be accommodated in the same transmission.

Brokers: Agents who specialize in bringing buyers and sellers together.

Browse: Feature of many database application programs by which files may be scanned for information of interest.

BSA: Blue Shield Association.

Budget Entity: Any accounting entity for which a budget is prepared.

Budget Performance Report: A periodic report from an organization's accounting function of the status of actual amounts or account totals compared to budgeted figures.

Budget Review Process: A systematic assessment of variances of financial operations from the operational budget.

Budget Variance: The difference between the anticipated amount for an item contained in a budget and the actual amount that results for that item during the period or any part thereof covered by the budget.

Budget: A financial plan based on predictions of future business operations. The budget lists in varying levels of detail an itemized account of anticipated receipts, disbursements, expenses, revenues, etc.

Budgeting: The process of developing a financial plan for an organization.

Buffer: An area of memory used to temporarily store data being transferred from one computer hardware device to another, such as data awaiting processing by a printer. Buffers are used to compensate for variations in the rates at which devices process data.

Bulk-Breaking: The division of larger quantities into smaller quantities as products or services get closer to the final market.

Bundling: Lumping related services together and charging one price instead of billing the services individually.

Burden of Proof: The responsibility in a legal proceeding of presenting sufficient evidence to prove a matter.

Burden: Indirect overhead expense.

Bus Network: A system by which linked computer workstations communicate through a common information distribution channel.

Business and Organizational Customers: Any buyers who buy for resale or to produce other goods and services.

Business Products: Products meant for use in producing other products.

Business Unit: An organization or organizational unit that is responsible for the production and marketing of a good or a service.

Buying Center: All the people who participate in or influence a specific purchase.

Buying Function: The position or department within an organization that is responsible for searching for and evaluating products and services.

Buying Market Share Strategy: Setting a low price in a price-conscious market to increase volume and generate new revenue.

Bylaws: See *medical staff bylaws*.

Byte: A grouping of eight bits processed by the computer as a unit. Bytes are the building blocks for characters in computer language.

C

C Corporation: The most common form of corporation recognized under the Internal Revenue Code. C corporations are taxable entities for income tax purposes. Their stockholders have limited liability for the debts of the corporation. See *S Corporation*.

CAD: Computer-assisted diagnosis, computer-assisted design.

Cafeteria Plan: Employee benefits plan under which beneficiaries may select from a menu of two or more benefits that include health benefits. Also called flexible benefits plans or flex plans.

CAI: Computer-assisted instruction.

Calendar Year Deductible: A deductible that applies to any medical expenses incurred by an insured during a calendar year.

Call: An option to purchase. The owner of the call has the right (but no obligation) to buy an asset or security at a specified price on (or before) a specified date. The writer of the call has the reciprocal obligation if the call is activated (exercised). The call provision (if any) of a bond gives the borrower (bond issuer) the right to redeem the bond for a dollar amount prior to its nominal maturity.

Call Premium: The extent to which the call price exceeds the face amount of a bond.

Call Price: The amount the bond issuer agrees to pay to redeem the bond prior to its nominal maturity date.

Cancelable Health Insurance Policy: An individual health insurance policy that may be terminated by the insurer at any time and for any reason by simply notifying the insured and refunding any advance premium that has been paid.

Capacity: The number of units of service or good that can be produced during a given period.

Capital (Cash) Flows: All disbursements and receipts between an organization and its capital suppliers (sources of financing).

Capital Asset: Physical facilities or equipment having long-term value. Such assets are carried on separate accounts, and their use is charged to current periods through depreciation expense.

Capital Budget: A plan for the acquisition of capital assets. It may include determination of sources of capital funds.

Capital Budgeting: The process of determining investment projects for an organization. The process may include determining the financial resources needed to establish and maintain expected cash inflows and outflows, and relating such needs to sources of capital.

Capital Claim: The claim a capital supplier has on the organization that received the capital, often evidenced by a security. Common stock or partnership interests are examples of equity claims; bonds are examples of debt claims.

Capital Gain: Under the Internal Revenue Code, the excess of proceeds over the cost basis of an asset that is sold. The designation of capital gain also includes a time element for which the asset must be held in order to qualify for preferential tax treatment.

Capital Infusion: In finance, a receipt in consideration of new debt or equity claims.

Capital Item: A long-lasting product that can be used and depreciated for many years.

Capital Lease: A noncancelable lease typically covering the full expected useful life of the leased asset. Maintenance of the asset is typically the responsibility of the lessor. The lessee treats the arrangement as both the borrowing of funds (incurring a liability) and the acquisition of an asset (which may be subject to depreciation). Both the liability and the asset are included on the balance sheet of the lessee. Contrast with *operating lease* and *net lease*.

Capital Structure: The percentages of various types of debt and equity that finance an organization.

Capital Supplier: A person or entity that supplies resources/money to an organization in an economic exchange in which the supplier agrees (by contract—liability—or by a residual claim—equity) to receive cash in the future as compensation for the value of the resources supplied.

Capital: In accounting, the owners' equity in or net worth of an entity, or an entity's fund balances as shown on the balance sheet; in economics and finance, all debt and equity, measured at market value, used to support (finance) the assets of an entity.

Capitalization Rate: Interest rate used to convert a series of payments into a present value.

Capitalization Ratio: See *debt ratio*.

Capitalization: To treat a current expenditure as an asset rather than as an expense for the period in which the expenditure was made.

Capitated (Health) Plan: A health insurance mechanism, such as an HMO, based on capitation.

Capitation: A set amount of money that is received or paid out on the basis of the total number of members or potential patients to be served rather than on the basis of those actually served or the actual services themselves. Usually expressed in units of "per member per month" (PMPM) and used by HMOs. Typically, capitation payments are made in advance of the period during which care is to be delivered. Hence, capitation is typically synonymous with prepayment.

Capped Fee Schedule: An approach used by PPOs and HMOs to set a maximum allowable fee for each procedure and service.

Career Management: Specific planned steps to achieve both short-term and long-term goals for an individual's professional and employment status. Also includes the setting of goals and routine monitoring of progress.

CARF: Commission on Accreditation and Rehabilitation Facilities.

Carrier: The insurer of a group contract who agrees to underwrite the policy's risk.

Carve-Out: Assignment of responsibility for financing and delivery of a specific subset of health care services to a separate provider network.

Case Law: The aggregate of reported decisions in cases on a particular legal subject.

Case Management: A utilization management function aimed at coordinating care to improve continuity and quality and reduce costs. A traditional term for all the activities that a physician or other health care professional normally performs to ensure coordination of the medical services required by a patient. It also, when used in connection with managed care, covers all the activities of evaluating the patient, planning treatment, referral, and follow-up so that care is continuous and comprehensive and payment for the care is obtained.

Case Manager: Person, often not a physician, responsible for developing, with appropriate clinicians, and implementing case management plans for individual patients.

Case Mix: The relative frequency and intensity of health care services, reflecting different needs and uses of resources. It can be measured on the basis of patient diagnoses (or severity of illnesses), utilization of resources, and provider characteristics.

Case-Mix Index: A weighted average of all patients discharged from the hospital that may vary by payer source. It is calculated by taking the sum of all DRG-related weights and dividing by the total number of discharges.

Case-Specific Claims Data: Information relating to the claims of an insured individual.

CASH: Commission for Administrative Services in Hospitals.

Cash Basis Accounting: An accounting method in which revenues are recognized only when payments are received and expenses are recognized only when disbursements are made.

Cash Budget: A financial plan, the focus of which is cash receipts and expenditures.

Cash Collateral: A cash or cash equivalent guarantee for a loan.

Cash Discount: A reduction in the stated or billed price of a good or service; typically allowed in consideration of prompt payment or volume purchases.

Cash Flow Equivalent: The value in money of an economic exchange in which no money passes from either party to the other at the time of the exchange. The simplest example is barter. The most common example is when resources are acquired by an organization and are simultaneously financed by the vendor of the resources.

Cash Flow Statement (sometimes Financial Cash Flow Statement): A finance (not accounting) statement that explains or forecasts various cash flows and cash flow equivalents for an organization; not the same as and in contrast with accounting's *statement of cash flows*.

Cash Flow: The receipt (inflow) or the disbursement (outflow or outlay) of cash by an organization.

Catastrophic Case: A patient who incurs disproportionately large medical expenses.

Catastrophic Health Insurance: Coverage for prolonged or severe illness that threatens the financial solvency of the insured.

Catastrophic Risk: A person with the potential for disproportionately large medical expenses.

Catchment Area: An HMO's geographic coverage area.

Cause and Effect Diagram: See fishbone chart.

Cause of Action: A set of facts or legal circumstances adequate to claim judicial attention.

CBO: Congressional Budget Office.

CCMM: Certifying Commission in Medical Management.

CD: See *certificate of deposit*.

CD-ROM: Off-line method of storing computer based information and files. The Compact Disc-Read Only Memory is capable of storing very large amounts of information, including complex graphical presentations.

CEA: Cost-effectiveness analysis.

Ceding Company: The company seeking reinsurance.

Cell: The storage dimension for a single unit of information, such as a bit, a byte, or a word. Also the location of a single entry of data in a computer spreadsheet.

Census: The number of patients in an inpatient facility at any given time.

Center of Excellence: A health care facility or network of facilities designated for provision of selected services on the basis of superior experience, outcomes, efficiency, and effectiveness.

Central Markets: Convenient locations where buyers and sellers can meet face-to-face to exchange products and services.

Central Planning Model: An economic system in which the allocation of resources is established by a government or government agency.

Central Processing Unit (CPU): Hardware and associated resident program instructions that control the interpretation and execution of all other instructions to the computer. Sometimes called the "brain" of the computer.

Central System: A single computer system that satisfies all of an organization's computing needs through use of common databases and interfaces.

Certificate: In group insurance, the document that is given to each insured to show type, amount, and beneficiary of coverage.

Certificate of Authority (COA): A state-issued certificate that allows an HMO to operate.

Certificate of Coverage: State-required description of the benefits provided in a health plan.

Certificate of Deposit (CD): An interest-bearing account at a financial institution that pays an interest rate commensurate with the period the holder agrees to maintain the account, usually several months to several years. A penalty typically is imposed for earlier withdrawal of the funds.

Certificate of Insurance: A document given to members of an insured group that outlines plan coverage and members' rights.

Certificate of Need (CON): A document issued by a state agency that authorizes a health care entity to build or expand facilities or services. Exact requirements of certificates vary among the states. CONs were initiated by the National Health Planning and Resources Development Act of 1974 (PL 93-641).

Certification: Any of the processes by which individual practitioners or institutions are deemed to meet rigorous performance standards for the provision of medical services.

Certiorari: A writ that commands a lower court to certify proceedings for review by a higher court. The writ is issued in order that the higher court may inspect the proceedings and establish if any legal irregularities have occurred. This is the common method of obtaining review of a case by the U.S. Supreme Court.

CHA: Catholic Health Association.

CHAMPUS: Civilian Health and Medical Program of Uniformed Services.

Change agent: An individual whose efforts facilitate change in a group of organizations.

Change-of-Occupation Provision: An individual health insurance policy provision that allows the insurer to change the premium of benefits when the insured changes jobs or career.

Channel Captain: A manager who helps direct the activities of a whole channel of distribution for products and services and tries to avoid—or solve—channel conflicts.

Channel of Distribution: Any series of firms or individuals who participate in the flow of products and services from producer to final user or consumer.

Channeling: The provision of economic incentives to patients, usually in the form of lower out-of-pocket payments or end-of-year bonuses, if those patients use particular health care providers.

Character Judgment: Evaluation of individuals in their capacity as moral agents. Expresses praise and blame for their actions.

Charge: See *price*.

Charge-Based Payment: Payment for services on the basis of typical charges to all patients.

Charges-to-Charges Ratio: See RCCAC.

Charitable Immunity: A now largely discarded legal doctrine under which charitable enterprises were held blameless for their negligent actions.

Charitable Trust: Assets administered by an independent trustee for charitable purposes.

Charity Care: Health care provided at no cost to the patient and with no expectation of reimbursement by a third-party payer.

Chart of Accounts: A listing of all accounts by number and name within broad categories (revenue, expense, inventory, capital, etc.) in accounting.

Chart: See *medical record*.

Checksheet: A data recording form that indicates how many times things have happened.

Chemical Dependency: Disorders characterized by abuse of alcohol and other drugs.

Child Abuse: Neglect or cruel treatment of a minor.

CHIN: Community health information network.

Chip: An electronic device that contains the circuitry and components that perform the computer's functions and serve as its memory.

Chorionic Villi Sampling: Procedure in which a catheter is passed vaginally into the uterus to draw fetal tissue from the placenta. Considered experimental, but shows promise as an alternative to amniocentesis.

Chronic Care: Care for patients with long-term illnesses.

Churning: The practice of providers' seeing patients more than medically necessary in order to increase revenue. The term may also apply to any performance-based reimbursement system with an emphasis on rewarding providers for seeing a high volume of patients.

Circumstantial Evidence: Testimony based on deduction from facts and not on personal, first-hand knowledge or observation.

Civil Law: The body of law that describes the private rights and responsibilities of individuals. It involves actions (e.g., in tort or contract) filed by one person against another. It does not encompass criminal law (crimes against society).

Claim: A request for payment under the terms of a policy.

Claimant: The person making a formal request for payment of benefits.

Claim Examiner: An insurance company employee who investigates claims to determine validity.

Claim Frequency Rate: The percentage of insureds expected to file claims.

Claim Lag: Time between provision of a service and submission of a claim. Also the time between submission of a claim and payment.

Claims Cost Assumption: Use of estimate of claims distribution around the mean in predicting risk. If the actual claims distribution is on target with the estimate, the good years will offset the bad years.

Claims Data: Information on patient treatment that is submitted to the managed care company at the time of the request for reimbursement.

Claims Distribution: A method of evaluating risk sharing within a specific population on the basis of actuarial risk principles. Involves construction of the distribution of claims around the mean.

Claims Processing: The steps required in moving from the submission of a claim to the distribution of payment.

Claims Review: Investigation of the validity of claims information.

Class Designation: A beneficiary designation that identifies a group rather than its individual members.

Class of Policies: All policies of a particular type or issued to a particular group of insureds.

Clayton Act: Antitrust legislation passed in 1914 to strengthen the provisions of the Sherman Act. 15 U.S.C. 12-27. The Act deals with price discrimination, exclusive dealing, tying arrangements, and mergers and acquisitions.

CLIA: Clinical Laboratories Improvement Act.

Clean Opinion: See *auditor's report*.

Client and Patient: A client gives consent for a procedure, assumes financial responsibility, and negotiates details. A patient is the recipient of the procedure. In medicine, the same person frequently fulfills both roles. However, children are considered patients, and their parents are clients.

Client Constituencies: Those people and organizations receiving or benefiting from the specific products of an organization: In a health care organization, the constituencies include (1) patients, those people who directly use health care services on an inpatient or an outpatient basis; (2) clients, people or organizations receiving services such as lab tests, blood, employee coverage, etc. from the organization, but not obtaining direct patient care; and (3) public, people who do not directly receive any services from the organization but who directly benefit, such as parents of children who are patients, etc.

Client Emphasis: Organizational focus on the needs of the client, viewing the product or service not as a specific unit (hospital, patient day, physician visit, hour of education) but in terms of what utility or benefit the client derives from it. All aspects of price (length of time before a patient can get an appointment, the time the client spends in the waiting room, the way the client is treated, and out-of-pocket expenses) are also considered.

Client Market: Everyone who has a significant probability of needing or using the organization's current or potential products or services.

Client Reporting: Provision to the consumer of information on utilization, costs, cost savings, and quality.

Client Server: See *server*.

Clinical Assessment System: A trademarked case management system from the New England Medical Center, Boston, Mass., that uses rule-based procedures to establish conditions that are indicative of clinical problems.

Clinical Decision Making: The process by which the clinician gathers data on a patient and his or her condition and arrives at a diagnosis, treatment program, and prognosis.

Clinical Disease Staging: A proprietary severity-of-illness indexing system offered by SysteMetrics/McGraw-Hill, Santa Barbara, Calif.

Clinical Grouping: Lumping services together for utilization review and other purposes in order to reflect the population at risk for services.

Clinical Guidelines: Protocols for clinical practice for particular treatments and procedures created by comparing current practices of physicians and selecting best practices. Also developed through review of scientific studies.

Clinical Integration: The extent to which the care a patient receives over time is coordinated across the functions and operating units of an organized delivery system. Clinical integration subsumes both horizontal and vertical integration.

Clinical Outcomes Management: The establishment of systems and standards for monitoring and measuring the quality of patient care on the basis of specific outcomes, such as health status, the occurrence or absence of specific clinical events, patient satisfaction, and other meaningful measures.

Clinical Pathway: See *critical pathway*.

Clinical Performance Monitoring: The process of monitoring the knowledge and skills of clinicians in terms of achievement of quantitative and/or qualitative standards in the provision of patient care.

Clinical Privileges: See *privileging*.

Clinical Quality: One of the elements, usually viewed as being a combination of scientific outcomes, quality of life outcomes, and service standards, in determining the acceptability of the patient care provided by a provider or a health care organization.

Clinical Rule: An accepted course of treatment or clinical decision.

CLMA: Clinical Laboratory Management Assocation.

Cloning: Producing an identical being from one somatic cell of its parent, or the asexual production of a progeny of an individual.

Close Corporation: A corporation, the stock of which is held by a small number of holders.

Close: In any sale, the point at which the salesperson requests an order from the buyer.

Closed Network: See *network*.

Closed Panel: A contracting arrangement under which physicians are tied exclusively to a single managed care entity.

Clustering Techniques: A variety of approaches used to find patterns within sets of data.

CME: Continuing medical education.

CMO: Chief medical officer.

CMP: Comprehensive medical plan.

COBOL: Common Business-Oriented Language for computers.

COBRA: Consolidated Omnibus Budget Reconciliation Act of 1985. Federal law that establishes conditions for the establishment and operation of employee benefit plans. Term used as shorthand for requirement that employees offer health insurance coverage to employees who lose coverage through termination or other reasons.

Code Creep: Intentional submission of claims using procedure codes that indicate more than was actually performed in order to obtain increased reimbursement.

Coded Disease Staging: See *Q-Stage*.

Coding System: Assignment of specific numerical identities to the full range of possible treatments and procedures.

Cognitive Dissonance: The state of anxiety or uneasiness that follows a decision and creates a need for reassurance that the decision was the best one. Also the tension that exists when two valid but contradictory analyses exist for a problem.

Coinsurance: A policy provision that requires the insured to pay a specified percentage or lump sum amount for the medical expenses for individual incidents of illness or injury.

Collaborative Reproduction: The contribution of a third party, a male sperm donor, or a surrogate mother in producing a human life.

Collateral: Assets pledged by a borrower to secure a loan.

Colleague Constituencies: All those people/organizations providing products or services similar to or related to those of the subject organization. In health care, appropriate constituencies might be other hospitals, physicians in independent practice, private laboratories, freestanding clinics, ambulatory care centers, public health departments, etc.

Collection Period: See *average collection period*.

Collections: In finance, a receipt from the sale of the organization's output (goods or services).

Coma Depasse: See *irreversible coma*.

Combined Target Market Approach: Combining of two or more submarkets into one larger target market as a basis for a single marketing strategy.

Combiners: Firms that try to increase the size of individual target markets by combining two or more market segments.

Combobox: A format commonly used in database data entry forms that constrains the user to a specific set of choices.

Command: A user-generated computer instruction.

Commercial Paper: Short-term, unsecured notes (corporate IOUs) issued to obtain working capital.

Commitment Fee: A payment to a lender to guarantee availability of loan funds at a future time.

Common Cause Variation: Variation caused by the interaction of a constant system of chance causes.

Common Law: Law that derives its authority from judicial decisions, as distinguished from law created by legislative enactment.

Communication: The exchange of transmission of ideas, attitudes, or beliefs between individuals or groups.

Community Rating: Establishment of an average premium in a specific geographic area. The costs of health care are thus spread evenly over an entire population.

Compact Disc Read-Only Memory (CD-ROM): Laser-based technology that permits the recording of large amounts of data on a single disk for later multiple readings by computer.

Comparative Advertising: Advertising that tries to develop selective demand for a specific brand rather than for a product or service category.

Compensation: The remuneration paid or benefits granted to an employee.

Compensating Balance: An amount required to be left by a borrower on deposit with the lender as a condition of a loan being made. The compensating balance effectively raises the interest rate for the loan.

Compensatory Damages: An award based upon the actual injury or loss sustained. The doctrine is designed to place the injured party in the same position he or she occupied prior to the injury and to provide nothing in addition.

Competency: The ability to make a rational decision. Also, an advanced level of knowledge or skill in a defined professional area.

Competition: The efforts of two or more commercial ventures to secure the business of third parties through the offering of more favorable terms.

Competitive Advantage: Attractiveness to potential buyers of one plan over another based on cost, benefits package, and other factors.

Competitive Analysis: An assessment by an organization of the performance of products or services of other organizations compared to that of its own products or services.

Competitive Barriers: The conditions that may make it difficult, or even impossible, for a firm to compete in a market.

Competitive Bids: Terms of sale offered by different suppliers in response to the buyer's purchase specifications.

Competitive Medical Plan (CMP): Federal designation that allows a plan to receive a Medicare risk contract without qualifying as an HMO.

Competitor Analysis: An organized approach for evaluating the strengths and weaknesses of current or potential competitors' marketing strategies.

Compiler: A program that translates high-level programming language (human language and symbols) into machine language.

Complaint: A document filed with the court by the plaintiff that sets out the authority of the court to hear the matter, the allegations of wrongdoing, the nature of the damages, and a request for relief. Alternatively, an expression of dissatisfaction by a customer regarding goods and/or services expected and/or provided.

Components: Items whose individual costs become part of a finished product's total cost.

Composite Rate: A standard premium available to everyone in a subscriber group regardless of the number of claimed dependents. Common among large employers and unions.

Compound Annuity Factor: The ratio of the value (cost) today of an annuity to the amount of the first payment of that annuity at a given interest rate.

Compound Interest: Calculation of interest on the basis of principal plus any previously unpaid (accrued) interest. Sometimes referred to as "interest on interest."

Compounding Factor: The ratio between the future and present values of a given amount of money held for a given number of periods at a specified interest rate, discount rate, required rate of return, etc.

Comprehensive Health Insurance Policy: A policy that contains both hospital-surgical and major medical benefits.

Comprehensive Major Medical Coverage: Complete and substantial major medical coverage in one policy, usually through a group health plan.

Comprehensive Care: Provision of a broad range of health care services required to prevent, diagnose, and treat illness.

Comprehensive Quality Management: One of several models, based on the total quality management approach, for management of overall quality in an organization.

Computer-Aided Instruction (CAI): The application of computers to educational programming.

Computer-Assisted Design (CAD): Use of computers and computer programs for image-driven, graphical fine-tuning of physical designs through a real-time trial-and-error process.

Computerized Medical Record: See *automated medical record*.

Computerized Severity Index (CSI): A proprietary severity-of-illness indexing system trademarked by Health Systems International, New Haven, Conn.

Concept Testing: A process for getting reactions from customers about how well a new product idea fits their needs.

Conceptual Damages: In litigation, all damages other than those that are economically formulated.

Concerted Refusals to Deal: See *boycott*.

Concurrent Authorization: Authorization of treatments or procedures at the time of diagnosis.

Concurrent Review: Assessment of a procedure or treatment at the time of provision by a professional other than the provider.

Conditional Receipt: A premium receipt that makes coverage effective only when a specified condition is met.

Conditionally Accredited: A designation used by the Joint Commission on Accreditation of Healthcare Organizations for hospitals that, during the accreditation process, fail to meet standards in a requisite number of areas. The hospitals have a specified period in which to meet standards or lose their accreditation altogether.

Conditionally Renewable Health Insurance Policy: A policy that grants the insurer the right to terminate coverage for reasons specified in the policy at the end of the policy term.

Confidentiality: Policy by which undesirable or unwanted disclosures of patient information is ensured. Generally, protection of information from disclosure.

Confirmatory Tests: Optional tests conducted to confirm death.

Conflict: A situation in interpersonal relationships in which individuals' positions on an issue are in such opposition that an impasse occurs. In the worse case, the impasse cannot be mediated and the conflict is long term. In most cases, mediation and/or negotiation will at least ameliorate the conflict.

Conflict of Interest: A situation in which private interests interfere with a person's ability to discharge official responsibilities.

Conjoint Analysis: A research technique that helps marketing managers determine how important certain elements of the firm's marketing mix are to target customers.

Consent: Authorization for an act by one who has the authority to provide it. See *informed consent*.

Consequential Damages: Losses or injuries that are the consequence of some act but are not the direct and immediate result of that act (also called special damages).

Consequentialism: Belief that an action is morally right if it is more right than wrong. See *utilitarianism*.

Consolidated Financial Statements: A combination of the individual financial statements of legally separate entities to show the economic condition of a single parent entity.

Conspiracy of Silence: A secret pact in which two or more people agree to keep quiet about a subject to achieve a common goal or to promote selfish interests. Also, an informal, unspoken agreement to ignore an issue.

Conspiracy: Concerted activity between or among separate economic entities. Includes not only express or written agreements, but also implied or tacit agreements proved by circumstantial evidence.

Constituency: A distinct set of people or organizations that is important to an organization's success and that is linked to the organization via exchange relationships.

Constructive Delivery: Relinquishing of control of the policy by the insurance company by physically delivering it to the policyowner or his or her agent.

Constructive Receipt: The addition of funds to an entity's income in the absence of any cash, e.g., interest amounts added on paper to savings or investment accounts.

Consultant Network: A group that HMOs contact when a referral must be made to a specialist.

Consultative Selling Approach: A type of sales presentation in which the salesperson develops a good understanding of the individual customer's needs before trying to close the sale.

Consumer Panel: A group of consumers who provide marketing information to a selling organization on a continuing basis.

Consumer Price Index (CPI): An index reported monthly by the Bureau of Labor Statistics of the U.S. Department of Labor. The index tracks the prices of selected goods and services. The CPI is issued for the overall U.S. economy and for various geographic regions as well as for many categories and subcategories of goods and services within the economy.

Consumer Product Safety Act: A 1972 federal law that set up the Consumer Product Safety Commission to encourage safety in product design and better quality control.

Consumer Products: Products meant for the final consumer.

Consumer Surplus: The difference between the value of a product or service to the consumer and the price the consumer pays.

Consumerism: A social movement that seeks to increase the rights and powers of consumers.

Consumption: The using up of goods, services, or other resources.

Contestable Period: The time during which the insurer may dispute the validity of a policy.

Contingency Reserve: A fund accumulated by an insurance company against unusual, unexpected events or conditions.

Contingent Liability: A potential liability, such as an unfavorable lawsuit outcome, that is listed in notes to a balance sheet rather than in the balance sheet accounts directly.

Continuance Tables: Statistics on distribution of claims according to duration of illness or amount of claims.

Continued Stay Review: Investigation of the appropriateness of the length of a hospital stay.

Continuity: The degree to which patient care is coordinated among providers and organizations and over time.

Continuous Quality Improvement (CQI): An approach to quality management by which all in an organization are fully involved in systems that monitor products and processes to ensure that they are provided at the best possible level of quality. CQI is an important element in the total quality management theory.

Continuum of Care: All health services provided in a single encounter or for multiple encounters over the lifetime of a patient.

Contraception: Prevention of conception or pregnancy.

Contract Administration: Use of an outside administrative organization for a managed care contract. For example, the administration by a utilization review organization of PPO contracts.

Contract Manufacturing: Marketing strategy by which production is relinquished to others but the marketing process is retained.

Contract Mix: Distribution of enrollees by numbers and categories of dependents. Contract mix is used to determine average contract size.

Contract Negotiations: The process by which the parties to a contract discuss, change, and agree to the terms of the contract.

Contract of Adhesion: A contract offered on essentially a "take-it-or-leave-it" basis under conditions where one party has so much more bargaining power than the other that the weaker party has no realistic choice as to the contract's terms. A court may refuse to enforce the contract if it finds that the weaker party has no choice but to agree to unconscionable terms.

Contract of Indemnity: A legal agreement in which the amount of benefit is based on the actual determination of financial loss.

Contract Profiling: Detailed report on the provisions and requirements of contracts.

Contract Size: The number of members in a contract.

Contractual Allowances: The difference between published or established prices for health care services and the amount that has been negotiated with a private third-party payer or imposed by a government third-party payer.

Contractual Channel Systems: Marketing approach in which distribution channel members agree to cooperate with one another.

Contrast Resolution: The number of bits per pixel in a graphic computer display. Used to measure the ability to distinguish screen or print-out intensity levels.

Contribution Margin: The percentage that the contribution represents of the amount collected.

Contribution: Actual collections net of variable costs. Also, the right of a party required to pay for an injury or loss to seek reimbursement from others who also caused the injury or loss. It is generally based on an apportionment of fault. For example, a physician against whom an award is sought may join another physician in the same or a later suit, alleging that the other physician is also responsible and should pay a percentage of the award based on his or her percentage of fault.

Contribution-Margin Approach: In cost analysis for a product or service, an approach in which functional costs are allocated in relationship to the quantity of the product or service produced.

Contributory Negligence: A portion of the responsibility for a compensable injury or loss ascribed to the plaintiff due to his or her own fault. Traditionally, it differs from comparative negligence in that it bars any recovery by the plaintiff (comparative negligence generally only reduces recovery by the plaintiff's percentage of fault).

Contributory Plan: A group insurance plan in which participants pay a portion of costs.

Control Chart: A graphic representation of a process over time that consists of a map of collected data on the process and the establishment of upper and lower control limits on the process. When the data collected on the process fall outside the control limits, the process is said to be out of control.

Control: An organization's system for ensuring that the conditions under which financial decisions are made and monitored are legally acceptable and in the best interests of the organization. In particular, the system should identify for managers variations between actual performance and plans or budgets. Also, the feedback process that helps the marketing manager learn how ongoing plans are working and how to plan for the future.

Controllable Cost: A cost that a particular manager can directly influence during a defined period.

Convenience Products: Products a consumer needs but isn't willing to spend much time or effort shopping for.

Conversion Privilege: The right of an individual insured under a group plan to convert from a group health policy to an individual policy if the person leaves the group. Also, the right to switch insurance plans regardless of age or physical condition.

Conversion: Movement of a member from group to individual coverage. This is a service to subscribers who lose group coverage through job loss, death of a spouse, etc. and can't obtain other group coverage.

Cookbook Medicine: Largely pejorative expression used by those opposed to rigid implementation of practice guidelines or parameters. The term references patient care provided "by the book."

Cooperative Advertising: Arrangement in which marketing middlemen and producers share the cost of ads.

Cooperative Chains: Groups formed by independent retailers to run their own buying organizations and to conduct joint promotion efforts.

Coordination of Benefits (COB) Provision: Policy specification that benefits will not be paid for expenses reimbursed by other insurers. Primary and secondary insurers are specified. The purpose of the specifications is to ensure that the insured receives no more than 100 percent of allowable medical expenses when multiple insurers are involved.

Coordination of Benefits: An agreement that prevents double payment for services when a subscriber has more than one insurance source. The agreement lays out which organization is responsible for payment and when.

Copayment: The amount of money collected from the insured or managed care patient for an encounter with the health care system, where the amount collected is calculated as a portion (fixed or percentage) of the total payment to the provider for that encounter.

Copy Thrust: The intended message of the words and illustrations of an ad.

Core Memory: Random-access portion of main memory that can be accessed directly by the central processing unit.

Corporate Bonds: Bonds issued by corporations.

Corporate Channel Systems: Maintenance of corporate ownership of all elements in the channel.

Corporate Liability: A growing body of the law that holds an organization responsible for the actions of those in its employ or of those with whom it holds a contractual relationship.

Corporation: A legal entity authorized to operate under the specific conditions of its state-granted charter.

Corrective Advertising: Ads placed, usually at the direction of regulatory agencies, to correct deceptive advertising.

Corridor Deductible: A flat amount above the hospital-surgical benefit that the insured must pay before major medical benefits take effect.

Cost: The sacrifice required of an individual or organization to acquire or produce a good or service, measured by the price of the good or service if acquired or by the dollar outlays or incurrence of debt of equity claims required for its production if produced.

Cost Accounting: That branch of accounting that focuses on the processes of classifying, summarizing, recording, reporting, and allocating expenses.

Cost Allocation: The assignment of portions of the cost of resources supporting or used by multiple activities within an organization to those activities, based on any formula deemed "equitable."

Cost-Based Reimbursement (CBR) or Cost-Based Payment: See *retrospective payment.*

Cost Basis: For purposes of income tax calculation pertaining to taxes related to gains and losses on the liquidation (sale or disposition) of assets, the portion of the proceeds from the liquidation that are not subject to taxation in accordance with applicable income tax rules.

Cost-Benefit Analysis: A method of comparing the cost of a program with its expected benefits in dollars (or other currency). The benefit-to-cost ratio is a measure of total return expected per unit of money spent. This analysis generally excludes consideration of factors that are not measured ultimately in economic terms. In contrast, cost-effectiveness analysis compares the benefits in nondollar terms (e.g., QALYs, deaths averted, cases prevented, etc.) with costs in dollars.

Cost-Benefit Approach: A technique for judging the appropriateness of services in which the benefits to patients are balanced against the cost of resources used to provide the services. The approach is an extension of the risk-benefit approach.

Cost Center: An area of business activity for which expenses are accumulated in accounting. Such centers typically receive revenue allocation or allocation of revenue that is greatly exceeded by expenses.

Cost Containment: Any strategy that is aimed at reducing health care costs and improving efficiency and effectiveness in service delivery.

Cost Containment Features: Premium reduction provisions that specify conditions that must be met before an insured qualifies for benefits.

Cost Contract: The agreement between the Health Care Financing Administration and a health plan for capitated payment for services to Medicare beneficiaries.

Cost Control: Any technique for ensuring that costs are maintained at budgeted levels or less.

Cost Effectiveness: The ratio of the cost of providing a health care product or service and the benefits to the patient of the product or service. Frequently expressed as cost per year of life of quality-adjusted life-year saved.

Cost-Effectiveness Analysis: A determination of the degree to which health benefits for a patient population are maximized for a given level of resource use, or the degree to which the use of resources is minimized in achieving a given benefit.

Cost Hierarchy: The various levels within an organization to which costs can be ascribed, ranging from the organization as a whole to an individual good or service.

Costing: The process of determining the costs of activities, goods, or services.

Cost Model: An actuarial pricing model from which actuarial assumptions may be drawn.

Cost Object: The level within the organization (see *cost hierarchy*) for which a separate cost determination is desired

Cost of Capital: The return as a percentage of capital (finance definition) that an organization must generate internally (before subsidies) in order to service that capital at a minimally adequate level. A cost of capital is typically defined for each class of capital having distinct service requirements. For example, separate costs of capital would be associated with each of the following: bank debt, bonds, and equity. The cost of capital is used as a discount rate to value internal cash flows related to a class of capital. See *social cost of capital* and *weighted average cost of capital.*

Cost of Sales: Total value in terms of producer's costs of the sales of products or services during a specified period.

Cost Pool: An aggregation of costs by good or service category, organizational division, or the like.

Cost Principle: Reporting the value of assets at historical or acquisition costs less accumulated depreciation.

Cost-Profit-Volume Analysis: For a given good or service produced by an organization, the determination of the relationships of cost and revenue behavior to volume. The analysis is done for a particular range of volume defined by the organization's capacity to produce the given good or service. The analysis permits identification of (1) "break-even points," if any, for that good or service, that is, the level(s) of volume, if any, at which total costs and total revenues are equal, and, hence, (2) ranges of volume in which profit or loss will be realized. Also known as "break-even analysis."

Cost Sharing: Partial payment by patients of health care costs under such methods as coinsurance, copayment, and deductibles.

Cost Shifting: Passing of unpaid costs of care to other payers.

Cost-to-Charges Ratio: See *RCCAC.*

Cost-Utility Analysis: The amount of satisfaction that is received from consumption of a product or service. In health care, determination of patient satisfaction with health care outcomes.

Count Data: The counting of occurrences of events, items, or units that have a particular characteristic.

Counterclaim: A claim brought by the defendant back against the plaintiff in the same suit and asserting an independent cause of action. The claim may be based on the same transaction or any other occurrence giving rise to a right of recovery by the defendant against the plaintiff. For example, a physician sued for malpractice may counterclaim for payment of his or her bill.

Covenants: Legal restrictions on the range of operations permitted for an organization under a contract or for an individual while working for or under contract with an organization. The provisions of bond indentures are examples of covenants. See *restrictive covenants*.

Covered Life: An insured individual, as in, "The typical insured household has 2.3 covered lives."

Covered Lives: The people to be covered under a health plan.

Covered Services: Items of care for a particular patient that are eligible for payment by a third-party payer under a contract.

CPE: Certified Physician Executive.

CPI: Consumer Price Index.

CPT: Current Procedural Terminology.

CPT-4 Classification (Current Procedural Terminology, 4th Edition): Five-digit codes for medical services that are used by providers in billing.

CQI: Continuous quality improvement.

Crash: Accidental or catastrophic shutdown of a computer due to hardware or user error.

Credentialing: A rigorous process by which a health organization ascertains that a clinician has acquired the knowledge and skills required for the provision of specific patient care. Partnered with the privileging process, credentialing ensures the organization that its clinicians are providing only care for which they are qualified.

Credit Rating: An assessment by a financial institution or a rating agency of the level of risk associated with extending a loan to a borrowing organization. See *bond rating*.

Credit: Any entry in accounting that records increases in revenue, equity, or liabilities, or decreases in expenses or assets. The opposite of debit.

Criminal Law: The body of law that deals with crimes, and their punishment, that are prosecuted by the state.

Critical Pathways: The best or ideal course of treatment or procedure for a specific disease or injury. Also called *clinical pathway* or care path.

Critical Processes: Those processes that are crucial to the quality of an organization's products or services and to meeting customers' needs.

Cross Claim: A claim brought by coplaintiffs or codefendants against each other rather than against a party on the opposite side of the litigation.

Cross-Examination: The examination of a witness by an adverse party—i.e., a party other than the one who has called the witness to render the testimony. The cross-examination follows the direct examination and is the primary tool for testing the accuracy of direct testimony.

Cross-Functional Team: A multidisciplinary approach to project and program management that draws participants from various organizational units as needed.

CSI: Computerized Severity Index.

Cultural Diversity: Coexistence of numerous distinct ethnic, racial, religious, or cultural groups within one social unit, organization, or population.

Cumulative Quantity Discounts: Reductions in price for larger purchases over a given period, such as a year.

Current Assets: Cash or assets that are expected to be converted into cash within the short term, usually a year. Typical current assets are cash, marketable securities, accounts receivable, inventory, and most prepayments.

Current Liabilities: Debts or obligations that must be honored in the short term, usually a year.

Current Procedural Terminology (CPT): A systematic listing of procedures and services provided by physicians. Mainly used for reimbursement purposes, but also plays an important role in research. Updated annually, the initialism is followed by the year of development.

Current Ratio: A financial ratio given by total current assets divided by total current liabilities.

Cursor: A blinking or otherwise highlighted indicator on the monitor screen of where the next character is to appear, where a correction is to be placed, or where the next piece of information is to be placed.

Custom-Designed: A computer system whose hardware and software are specific to the organization in which they are used.

Customer Service Level: Staffing (for services) and inventory (for products) that determine how rapidly and dependably a firm can deliver what customers want.

Customer-Centered Organization: An organization that makes every effort to sense, serve, and satisfy the needs and wants of its clients and publics within budgetary constraints.

Cut and Paste: A technique in many word processing and graphic application programs by which groups of words or images can be moved intact to a new location.

Cut-Off Rate: See *hurdle rate*.

CV: Curriculum vitae.

Cycle of Continuous Improvement: The view of the quality improvement process as a continuous loop of assessment of problems, improvement planning, implementation, and evaluation of results, followed by further problem assessment.

D

Daily Census: See *census*.

Damages: The monetary recovery allowed by the law. Generally described as either compensatory or punitive. See *compensatory damages* and *punitive damages*.

Darling v. Charleston Community Hospital: Ground-breaking court decision that held in 1965 that a hospital was legally responsible for ensuring that its medical staff had the requisite knowledge and skills to provide care within its walls.

Database: A collection of stored data and the organizational logic of their storage pattern.

Database Management System (DBMS): The set of programs that provides access to and allows manipulation of databases.

Data Bus: A system that connects the central processing unit, data storage elements, and all peripheral devices for the exchange of data within a computer system.

Data Commissions: See *state data commissions*.

Data Management: All of the functions necessary for the computerized organizing, cataloging, locating, retrieving, storing, and maintaining of data.

Date Back: See *back-date*.

DATTA: Diagnostic and Therapeutic Technology Assessment.

Days in Accounts Receivable: See *average collection period*.

dBase: A popular commercial database management software package that allows access to multiple files in the database simultaneously and design of screen fields that are user-specific.

Dealer Brands: Brands created by channel elements between the producer and the ultimate user—sometimes referred to as private brands.

Death Spiral: The alternating imposition of increased premiums and subsequent adverse selection that can place a carrier in a permanent loss position.

Death: Defined variously as total stoppage of the circulation of blood and bodily functions. *See Brain Death* and *Uniform Determination of Death Act.*

Debenture: A bond not covered by collateral.

Debit: Any entry in accounting that records increases in expenses and assets and decreases in revenues, liabilities, and equity. The opposite of credit.

Debt Ratio: Any of a number of financial ratios (e.g. debt-to-assets ratio, debt-to-equity ratio) that provide some indication of the financing structure of the organization.

Debt Supplier: A capital supplier accepting a debt claim in exchange for capital supplied.

Debt-to-Assets Ratio: A financial ratio given by total liabilities divided by total assets of an organization.

Debt-to-Equity Ratio: A financial ratio given by total liabilities divided by net worth of an organization.

Debugger: A system program that allows programmers to locate and correct errors in programming.

Decider: In the exchange process, the person who chooses between alternatives that will satisfy a want or need.

Decision Support System: Generally used to describe computer-based data acquisition and analysis systems used to make clinical decisions about patients' conditions.

Decision Tree: In clinical decision making, the process of moving from a general diagnosis to more and more specific evaluation of the patient's injury or condition. A graphic presentation of an algorithm.

Declining Market: A market in which the quantity of exchanges is diminishing and appears likely to continue doing so.

Decoder: The receiver in the communication process and the point at which messages are translated.

Deductible Expense: Any expense that may be subtracted from revenues before computing income tax liabilities.

Deductible: A level of total payment that must be made by a subscriber or policyholder before an insurer or managed care organization assumes any responsibility for payment.

Deduction: See allowance.

De Facto: A right or obligation established as a matter of custom or common conduct and not founded upon a statute or common law.

Defamation: Untrue statements that have the effect of injuring the reputation or good name of another party. Oral defamation is known as slander; written defamation is libel.

Default Risk: Potential for an organization to fail to pay principal and/or interest on a loan at the designated time.

Defendant: The party against whom a criminal complaint has been made or against whom recovery or relief is sought in a lawsuit.

Defensive Medicine: The ordering by a clinician of tests and procedures more for their likely impact on a patient's tendency to litigate a negative result than for their appropriateness in the treatment of the patient's condition or injury.

Deficit: A negative balance in any revenue or income account.

Deflation: A condition of generally declining prices for goods and services.

De Jure: "As a matter of law"(contrast with *de facto*).

Demand Curve: A graph of the relationship between price and quantity for a range of possible quantities demanded in a market, assuming all other things stay the same.

Demand Deposit: Funds in a checking account at a depository institution such as a bank, so-called because the funds may be withdrawn at any time (on demand).

Demand: The quantity of a good or service consumers are willing to acquire at a given price.

Demand-Backward Pricing: Marketing strategy in which an acceptable final consumer price is set and the producer's price to the channel is calculated working backward.

Demand Management: Information-based strategies for ensuring that consumers make health care decisions that lead to effective and efficient use of services.

Deming Cycle: See *plan-do-check-act cycle*.

Deming Prize: Given by the Japanese government and named for the founder of the total quality management approach, W. Edwards Deming, this annual prize honors outstanding corporate quality.

Demographic Risk: Adjustment for the demographic characteristics of the members enrolled in an HMO.

Demographic Segmentation: Grouping of potential insureds according to statistical characteristics.

Demographics: Statistics about a population, such as sex, age, marital status, birthrate, mortality rate, education, income, and occupation.

Demurrer: A formal objection by one of the parties to a lawsuit that the evidence presented by the opponent is insufficient to justify the lawsuit. Federal Rules of Civil Procedure, Rule 12 (b)(6), allows a party to move for dismissal because of the other party's failure to state a claim upon which relief can be granted.

Deontology: Ethical analysis according to a moral code or rules that does not take into consideration consequences of actions. The Golden Rule is an example.

Deployment Chart: The timetable for introducing a total quality management program to an organization that shows the individuals or groups responsible for each process in the organization.

Deposition: A procedure used in preparing for litigation whereby the witness is placed under oath and either side is afforded the opportunity to question him or her. Depending on the rules of the jurisdiction, the testimony may be presented as evidence or used to undermine the testimony of the witness during trial.

Depreciable Amount: The value or portion of the value of an asset that may be subjected in the accounting process to rules or laws/regulations related to depreciation.

Depreciable Assets: Any resources that may be subjected in the accounting process to the rules or laws/regulations related to depreciation.

Depreciable Life: The period over which a depreciable cost of an asset is expensed.

Depreciation: A reduction in the economic worth of an asset. In accounting, a process for allocating the cost of an asset to the periods of its use. A number of different depreciation methods may be used: annuity, composite, compound interest, declining balance, percentage (>100 percent) declining balance, replacement, retirement, straight line, sinking fund and sum-of-the-years-digits.

Deregulation: Removal of restrictions on business activities through legislation or through elimination of formal regulations.

Derivative: Any investment the value of which is based on (derived from) other assets or investments. Examples of derivatives include *calls* and *puts*.

Derived Demand: Demand for business products that derives from the demand for final consumer products.

Description (Specification) Buying: Purchases made on the basis of a written or oral description of the product or service rather than the product or service itself.

Descriptive Ethics: Factual investigation of moral behavior and beliefs.

Desktop Computer: A complete computer system, including all peripheral units, that fits on a desktop. Commonly used to describe computerized production of printed and published materials.

Detoxification: Medical supervision of the process of withdrawing a patient from alcohol or other substance abuse addiction.

DHEW: Department of Health, Education, and Welfare (now DHHS).

DHHS: Department of Health and Human Services.

Diagnosis Codes: Numerical identities assigned to medical services for ease in billing.

Diagnosis-Related Groups (DRGs): A system for classifying hospital inpatients having similar demographic, diagnostic, and/or treatment characteristics into groups within which each patient is expected to have relatively homogeneous use of resources for treatment. Groups are established for the purpose of generating a rate or fee schedule comprising a single payment for each group independent of actual resource use by each patient in the group. Groups may also be used to estimate the relative intensity of patient treatment across providers. Medicare was the first large payer to use DRGs and did so for inpatient services, basing its definitions of DRGs on the assumption that length of stay was a reasonable surrogate for resource use.

Diagnostic and Statistical Manual of Mental Disorders (DSM-IV): A manual used to provide a diagnostic coding system for mental and substance abuse disorders.

Diagnostic Cost Groups (DCGs): A listing that incorporates the prior hospitalization experience of people when they enroll in an a health maintenance organization.

Dicta: The commentary of a judge in a written opinion that indicates his or her feelings on the matters under discussion but that is not necessary to the decision in the case. Dicta are not binding on courts in subsequent cases. (see holding)

Digital Data: Information expressed in the form of numerical digits.

Dilution: A reduction in the value of a security or other financial holding that results from an increase in the number of fungible units of the financial device outstanding.

Diminishing Marginal Returns: The economic concept that the marginal (incremental) value of a unit of output is inversely related to the existing quantity of that output before the increment is added. For example, a rural community realizes more value from the first primary care provider to move to the community than from the second, given the presence of the first.

Direct Advertising: Competitive advertising that aims for immediate buying actions.

Direct Contract Model: A health plan that contracts directly with private practice physicians. Common in open-panel HMOs.

Direct Costs: The cost of labor, materials, and other resources that can be identified with and result from producing a specific good or service. Contrast with *indirect costs*.

Direct Evidence: Means of proof that tends to show the existence of a fact in question, without the intervention of the proof of any other fact. Direct evidence is distinguishable from circumstantial or indirect evidence. See *circumstantial evidence*.

Direct Examination: The questioning of a witness by the party who has called the witness to render testimony. It is generally the first interrogation and is followed by a cross-examination conducted by the opposing party.

Direct Marketing: Direct communication between a seller and an individual customer using a promotion method other than face-to-face personal selling. Also, situation in which an HMO deals directly with an employer.

Directory: In a computer, the partitioning of operating system and data files into distinct collections. Also used to describe the index of these files. Directories may be further divided into a hierarchy of subdirectories for both volume and logic reasons. Directories and subdirectories of computer files are equivalent to physical filing cabinets or cabinet drawers.

Direct Placement: The sale of a bond or other security by private negotiation, typically to a single investor.

Direct Standardization: In severity indexing methods, the use of provider-specific rather than general population outcomes data to determine risk-adjustment factors.

Directed Verdict: An order of the court that may be issued at the request of either party at the conclusion of the opposing party's presentation of evidence or at the conclusion of the trial. It is a determination by the trial judge that the evidence or law so clearly favors one party that it is pointless for the trial to proceed. The judge decides that one side or the other is entitled to a judgment as a matter of law, taking the issue out of the hands of the jury. The conclusion of the judge should be so obvious that reasonable minds could not arrive at a differing conclusion. For example, the defendant physician, at the conclusion of the plaintiff's case, may move for a verdict in his or her favor (a directed verdict) based on an assertion that the plaintiff has failed to present sufficient evidence upon which a jury could return a verdict for the plaintiff.

Disallowance: Denial of all or part of a claim by a health care payer.

Disbursement: An outlay or payment made by cash, check, or by cash flow equivalent, regardless of the purpose or objective of the payment.

Discharge Abstracts: See *Uniform Hospital Discharge Data Set.*

Discharge Data: Information that is collected on patients when they are discharged from the hospital.

Discharge Planning: Planning for care that will be needed when the patient leaves the hospital, such as home health care. The purpose of discharge planning is to move patients from the hospital at the earliest possible time consistent with high-quality health care delivery and to the most effective and least costly alternative site of care.

Disciplinary Procedures: The chronological and intensity steps that are specified in an organization's by-laws for dealing with a clinician who fails to meet acceptable standards of performance or behavior.

Discounted Cash Flow: The present value of future cash flows using an appropriate discount rate(s). Alternatively, it is the present amount of money that would have to be invested at a given interest rate to grow to a given amount at some future time.

Discounted Fee for Service: Agreement by provider to provide services under a specified discount from usual charges.

Discounting: (1) Reduction in the established price of a good or service on the basis of volume or frequency of purchase, of rapid payment, or of any other reason determined by the seller; (2) the process of calculating discounted cash flow.

Discount Rate: The rate, based on the risk attached to the accuracy of future cash flows, used in calculating the present value of those cash flows.

Discounts: Reductions from list prices given by sellers to buyers. Also, reductions negotiated in customary charges.

Discovery: The formal process of obtaining information in preparation for litigation. It requires notice to all parties and an equal opportunity for all parties to obtain the information. It is distinguishable from the informal investigations conducted by one side or the other in preparing a case in that formal discovery allows the parties to use the power of the court to compel revelation of testimony or documents that may be under the exclusive control of the other party. For example, a subpoena may be issued to compel a witness to testify at deposition as a part of the discovery process.

Discrepancy of Assortment: Difference between the lines a typical producer offers and the assortment final consumers or users want.

Discrepancy of Quantity: The difference between the quantity it is economical for a producer to offer and the quantity final users or consumers normally want.

Discretionary Income: What is left of disposable income after necessities are paid for.

Discretionary Medicine: Benefits that people choose to add and pay for beyond the basic benefits package offered.

Disease Classification: A statistical approach in which related diseases are listed in a limited number of categories for research or payment purposes.

Disease Management: A comprehensive, integrated approach to care and reimbursement based on the natural course of a disease, with treatment designed to address the illness by maximizing the effectiveness and efficiency of care delivery. The emphasis is on preventing disease and/or managing it aggressively where intervention will have the greatest impact.

Disease Prevention (Wellness): Keeping healthy people from getting sick by monitoring them while they're well.

Disenrollment: Termination of coverage by a member or insured or by the plan or insurer. The latter termination is usually severely proscribed by state or federal law. The former is an important gauge of customer satisfaction with health plans.

Disincentives: An approach to discourage enrollees from receiving eligible services from a non-network provider.

Disk. A magnetic device for storage of information and programs for computers.

Dismissal with Prejudice: The termination of a lawsuit without the right to reinstitute the proceeding.

Dismissal without Prejudice: The termination of a lawsuit that preserves the right to reinstitute the proceedings.

Dispensing Fee: A fee charged for prescription drugs. Contracts generally separate payment into two segments: the medication's average wholesale price and the dispensing fee.

Disposable Income: Income that is left after taxes.

Disproportionate Share: Refers to catastrophic risk where a small population uses an excessive amount of medical resources.

Dissonance: Tension caused by uncertainty in choosing between two or more alternatives.

Distributed System: A collection of independent computers that share data, programs, and other resources, such as printers, scanners, modems, and other peripheral components.

Distribution Center: A special kind of warehouse designed to speed the flow of goods and avoid unnecessary storing costs.

Distributive Justice: Spreading benefits and burdens among everyone. In the health care setting, the term reflects the way resources and money are allocated.

Disvalue: Disregard; assign a negative value to an action or result.

Diversification: Strategy of moving into totally different lines of business—perhaps entirely unfamiliar products, markets, or even levels in the production-marketing system. Also a strategy for maintaining growth in a period in which existing product lines are stagnant.

Divestment: In finance, the sale or liquidation of an asset; also the receipt generated by the sale or liquidation of an asset.

Dividend: Distribution of earnings to owners of a corporation in the form of cash, stock, property, or other securities. Dividends other than distributions of stock become an organizational liability at the time they are declared. Also, a premium refund made to the holder of a group insurance policy when the group's claim experience is better than that anticipated when the premium rate was established.

Do Not Resuscitate (DNR): An order given to either discontinue or not initiate medical treatment for a patient who would not benefit from it or at the request of a patient who would benefit but chooses not to have "heroic measures" performed. Both areas of DNR are controversial to some degree because of varying ability to define specific situations in which the orders are given.

Doctor/Patient Privilege: Originally created as a rule of evidence by some jurisdictions to preclude the introduction into evidence of information disclosed or obtained by the physician in the course of the doctor/patient relationship. The concept has been expanded in a number of jurisdictions to preclude such disclosure, whether in or out of court, to any unauthorized person.

Document: See *file*.

DOS (Disk Operating System): A specialized program, installed in main memory during booting, that provides a link between the user and the computer's disk drives, both floppy and hard.

Dot Matrix Printer: A printer that creates characters and graphics by imposition of dot patterns. The quality of printing is determined by the number of dots used in each print field. This technology has largely given way to laser and other more advanced printing technqiues.

Double Effect: To satisfy this moral principle, the following conditions must be met: the action must not be intrinsically wrong; only the good effect must be intended; the good effect must be achieved by the act, not by way of the bad effect; and the good result must override the evil.

Download: Process of transferring data or programs from a computer to another computer, to a storage medium, to a printer, or to any other device.

Dread Disease Policy: See *limited coverage policy*.

DRG: See *diagnosis-related groups*.

Drive: Hardware components necessary for transferring data to and from a floppy disk. Also, a strong stimulus that encourages action to reduce a need.

Driver: Software instructions that the computer follows to format data for transfer to printers and other peripheral devices. In marketing, the market elements or agents that create and/or sustain growth in the demand for a product or service.

Drug Screening: Testing used to determine the presence of drugs and to measure the amount of drugs in an individual's system.

Drug Use Evaluation (DUE): Evaluation of the prescribing patterns of physicians to assess appropriateness of drug therapy.

Drug Utilization Review (DUR): Systematic analysis of the appropriateness and effectiveness of the use of specific medications for specific disease and injury states. An important element in the construction and maintenance of a drug formulary.

Dual Distribution: Use by a producer of several competing channels to reach the same target market, such as use of several middlemen in addition to direct sales.

Dual Option: The offering of both an HMO and a traditional insurance plan.

Due Process: The right of fundamental fairness in proceedings that are judicial or quasi-judicial in nature (also known as procedural due process). Due process ensures those subject to such proceedings that they are being dealt with according to generally understood rules and regulations. Due process clauses are found in the 5th and 14th Amendments of the U.S. Constitution and in most state constitutions. These clauses protect the individual from federal or state governmental actions that are arbitrary or unfair. Substantive due process refers to evaluation of laws to see that they are rationally related to a legitimate goal.

Due Process Requirement: Mandate for objective criteria in selecting or terminating preferred providers. Prohibits discrimination among classes of providers that has nothing to do with their performance.

Dumb Terminal: A visual display terminal and keyboard with minimal input/output capability and no processing capability.

Dumping: Pricing a product sold in a foreign market below the cost of producing it or at a price lower than that used in its domestic market. Also, rejecting or transferring a patient to another provider because of the patient's presumed inability to pay for services.

DUR: Drug utilization review.

Durable Medical Equipment (DME): Equipment, such as wheelchairs, that is used repeatedly in the treatment of medical conditions.

Durable Power of Attorney: A legal instrument that authorizes an individual to act on another's behalf. When authorized for medical decision-making, it is considered a form of *advance directive* and allows a party to make treatment decisions for a patient lacking decision-making capacity.

Duty: A legally enforceable obligation owed by one to another. For purposes of civil liability, it is distinguishable from a moral obligation, which is not generally enforceable at law.

Duty to Account: The obligation of an agent or employee to maintain accurate financial records and to turn over any funds or properties received on behalf of an employer or contractor.

Dynamic Data Exchange (DDE): An established protocol for exchanging data through active links between applications that run under Microsoft Windows®.

E

Early Adopters: The second group in the *adoption curve* to adopt a new product; these people are usually respected by their peers and often are opinion leaders.

Early Intervention: Monitoring healthy people so problems and diseases can be caught early and treated less extensively. Also, specific programs aimed at discovering developmental delays in children.

Early Majority: A group in the *adoption curve* that avoids risk and waits to consider a new idea until many early adopters try and like it.

Earnings: Most commonly refers to net income or profits.

Econometrics: The application of statistical methods to the study of economic data and problems.

Economic Competition: The effort of two or more parties to secure the business of a third party by offering, usually under fair or equitable rules of business practice, the most favorable terms.

Economic Credentialing: The process of judging a clinician's fitness to provide care in an organization on the basis of the historical costs versus profits or losses associated with the clinician's practice patterns.

Economic Damages: Those elements of injury or loss that can be easily and accurately calculated in terms of money damages. These include such items as the cost of medical care and lost wages. Economic damages are distinguishable from noneconomic damages (e.g., pain and suffering), which cannot be calculated with the same accuracy.

Economic Exchange: Any transaction in which each party surrenders something of value to the other party. For example, one party gives up assets (money, goods, or services) or incurs a liability or claim in exchange for receiving from the other party an asset or relief from a liability or claim.

Economic Life: The period during which benefits are expected to be derived from an asset.

Economic Needs: Needs concerned with making the best use of a consumer's time and money, in the consumer's judgment.

Economic Order Quantity: In inventory management, a reorder quantity that is based on a balance among (1) the cost of maintaining a stock of inventory, (2) the cost of placing orders, and (3) the cost of running out of inventory (stocking out).

Economic Profit: See *net present value*.

Economic Stabilization Program: A federal program of the 1970s that was aimed at reducing inflation through the imposition of selective wage controls and price controls.

Economies of Scale: The tendency for the per-unit cost (average cost) of a good or service to decrease with increasing volume as fixed costs are spread over a larger number of units.

Education-Based Resource Management: A philosophical approach to providing individualized feedback to providers in an educational setting in order to improve clinical decision making.

Effectiveness: A measure of the degree to which a diagnosis, treatment, or procedure leads to the desired or anticipated outcome for the patient and is provided in the correct manner. See *efficacy* and *efficiency*.

Effectiveness in Exchanges: The belief that constituencies that are targets of marketing efforts become more satisfied with current exchanges and more receptive to new exchanges.

Efficacy: A measure of the degree to which a diagnosis, treatment, or procedure, under ideal or research conditions, is capable of providing desired results for a specific disease or injury. For researchers, efficacy is the demonstrated effect of a treatment in a clinical trial, whereas effectiveness is the demonstrated effect of a treatment in general usage (i.e., not in a controlled trial). See *effectiveness* and *efficiency*.

Efficiency: The degree to which the costs of input resources are minimized for a defined output, or the value of outputs is maximized for a given cost of input resources.

EGA (Enhanced Graphics Adapter): A display technology for the personal computer; it has now been replaced by VGA.

Egalitarian Theory: Emphasizes equal access to things in life that all rational people desire. Also, a social philosophy that espouses removal of inequalities among people.

Eighty-Twenty (80\20 Rule): A general principle that, in marketing, refers to the fact that a large percentage of a company's sales and profits comes from a relatively small percentage of its customers or products. See *heavy half, Pareto principle*.

Elastic Demand: Economic principle that states that, if prices are changed, the quantity demanded of a product or service will change in the other direction enough to increase/decrease total revenue.

Elastic Supply: Economic principle that states that the quantity of a product or service supplied changes more if the price is raised than if it is lowered.

Elective Procedure: Any surgical procedure not deemed of immediate need for a patient.

Electronic Data Interchange (EDI): A protocol for creating common data definitions for the purpose of exchanging business-related data elements.

Electronic Patient Record: See *automated patient record.*

Electronic Mail: The process of sending, receiving, storing, and forwarding messages between users on a telecommunications or local area network.

Electronic Spreadsheet: A program typically operated on a personal computer that is used to facilitate budgeting or financial planning.

Eligibility: The ability to obtain health insurance coverage.

Eligibility Data: Information on patients' past histories that managed care companies use to determine whether someone is eligible for coverage.

Eligibility Period: In contributory plans, the period during which a new employee may apply for coverage.

Eligibility Requirements: The conditions that must be met for participation in a group plan.

EMCRO: Emergency medical care review organization.

Emergency Products: Products that are purchased immediately when the need is great.

Emergicenter: A specialized health care facility that provides short-term care for urgent conditions.

Employee Assistance Program (EAP): A program operated by employers to help employees overcome such things as alcohol and substance abuse problems and mental health problems before they require medical treatment.

Employee Risk Profile: Report on the past health experiences of workers.

Employee Stock Ownership Plan (ESOP): Any of several arrangements under which employees of an organization acquire ownership interests in the organization.

Empowerment: Acknowledgment of the responsibility of employees and granting to them the authority to do their jobs without unnecessary or cumbersome supervision. An essential ingredient of total quality management, empowerment gives employees optimum ownership of their jobs.

Enabling: Providing the means, opportunity, power, or authority for an individual to take an action.

Encoding: Process by which the source in the communication process decides what it wants to say and translates it into words or symbols that will have the same meaning to the receiver.

Encumbrance: Funds reserved for use in specific expenditures for which a commitment has been made even though there has been no performance that would require the expenditures yet. For example, a fund might be established to cover the cost of goods ordered but not yet delivered.

Endorsement: See *rider*.

Endowment: A donation in which the donor stipulates that the principal must remain in perpetuity, with only the interest available to the donee.

Engaged Market: Situation in which market exchanges are occurring, but with a competitive organization.

Enrollee Choice Patterns: Information used to determine which type of coverage enrollees want.

Enrollee: Person covered under a health care plan.

Enrollment Information: Information collected prior to enrolling people in a plan.

Enrollment Period: A period set by the managed care company to accept new plan members.

Entitlement: Right to benefits as spelled out in a contract.

Entitlement Programs: Any of several federal, state, or local government programs that provide benefits to specified groups of citizens who qualify for those benefits under the programs' enabling legislation. Examples include Medicare and Medicaid, at the federal and state levels, respectively.

Environment: A set of forces external to the organization that the marketer may be able to influence but cannot control.

Environmental Assessment: The process of compiling data necessary to evaluate the consumer market for a new plan. It includes projected population growth, economic conditions, labor supply, hospitalization rates, etc.

Epidemiological Analysis: Use of traditional epidemiological techniques to measure outcomes in given populations and thus determine the effectiveness of care (i.e., observational studies such as cohort studies or case-control studies).

EPSDT: Early periodic screening, diagnosis, and treatment.

Equal Contribution Rules: The requirement that an employer's contribution to a federally qualified HMO plan be equal to the largest contribution paid on behalf of the employee to a non-HMO plan.

Equality: The state of being equal.

Equilibrium Point: The point at which the quantity and the price sellers are willing to offer are equal to the quantity and the price buyers are willing to accept.

Equity: Freedom from bias; justice according to natural law. Also, legal rules and doctrines developed to add to or override existing rules or doctrines to protect human rights. Also, An ownership or residual claim on the assets of an organization, subordinate to debt claims. Also a source of capital.

Equity Security: A share in a corporation, an ownership interest in a limited partnership, or any rights to such shares or interests.

Equity Supplier: A capital supplier accepting an equity claim in exchange for the capital supplied.

Erase: The removal of data or commands from a computer record.

Ergonomics: An applied science dealing with considering the characteristics of people in order to achieve the safest and most effective interaction between them and the workplace.

ERISA: Employee Retirement Income Security Act of 1974. Federal law and regulations that govern the establishment and operation of company pension and other employee benefits programs.

Ethical Fundamental Review Criteria: Selection and prioritization of patients' rights, human values, and other ethical issues in order to tailor care to the individual.

Ethicist: One who can classify, diagnose, and suggest solutions for moral problems. In a hospital, an ethicist provides staff education, aids in policy formation, and consults on clinical cases.

Ethics: A system of values that guides behavior in particular roles. Different roles call for different ethical standards. Professional ethics are defined by ethical standards and codes and are established expectations that professional people follow and upon which their behavior can be evaluated.

Ethics Committee: A broad-ranging group assembled to form a consensus for resolution of ethical problems and issues and to assist in bioethical decision and policy making. See *institutional ethics committee*.

Ethics Grand Rounds: Review and discussion of ethical and value issues of patients and how they may affect treatment.

Eugenics: The science of increasing the frequency of desirable genes and decreasing the frequency of undesirable genes.

Euthanasia: Mercy killing, generally considered homicide, or the act of permitting the death of a terminally ill person. See *passive euthanasia*.

Evaluative Judgments: Concerned with what is worthwhile or valuable to have or do. Used in goal-setting.

Exchange: The basis for the relationship between an organization and its constituents and markets, either real or potential. Exchanges are typically goods, services, or money, each representing utility or benefit to the parties in the exchange.

Exclusion Rider: A attachment to a policy that specifies conditions for which no benefits will be paid.

Exclusions: Expenses specifically not covered by a policy.

Exclusive Contract: A form of agreement whereby one person or entity contracts with a second person or entity for provision of a particular service or product and agrees that no other person or entity will be permitted to render a similar service or provide a similar product.

Exclusive Contracting: Situation in which physicians establish an IPA and no longer compete with each other. To avoid antitrust problems, the rule of thumb is for no more than 20 to 30 percent of area physicians to form such an IPA. More

Exclusive Dealing Arrangement: Arrangements in which a buyer agrees not to deal in any goods or services that compete with those of the seller.

Exclusive Distribution: Use of only one middleman in a particular geographic area.

Exclusive Provider Organization (EPO): Similar to preferred provider organization, except subscribers are limited to participating providers.

Executive Committee: See *medical staff executive committee*.

Exemplary Damages: Punitive damages. A sum of money awarded not to compensate the injured party, but to punish the guilty party and deter him or her and others from similar acts. It generally requires that the defendant act in a willful, wanton, or reckless fashion.

Exercise Price: See *option*.

Exhaustion of Remedies: A legal doctrine that requires a plaintiff to exhaust all nonjudicial remedies (e.g., administrative hearings and appeals) before pursuing a lawsuit.

Expenditure: In finance, a disbursement for the acquisition of resources, goods, or services expected to be used, consumed, or sold in the short term.

Expense Item: A product or service whose total cost is treated as a business expense in the period that it's purchased.

Expense Participation: Deductibles, coinsurance, and other techniques for requiring the insured to pay some portion of his or her medical expenses.

Expense: The recognition in accounting of the cost of the resources used in the generation of revenue. It is sometimes referred to as an "expired cost."

Experience Curve Pricing: Pricing technique that uses an estimate of future average costs based on past experience.

Experience Rating: The setting of health insurance premiums on the basis of specific attributes of the insured person(s), including claims history and health status.

Experience Refund: See *dividend*.

Experience Tracking: Gathering the information to establish an experience rating.

Experimental Design: A technique for improving a process or system by reducing or shifting common cause variation. The technique is used to determine the most resource-efficient method of eliminating process variation.

Experimental Medical Care Review Organization (EMCRO): One of the earlier forms of federal peer and care review organizations. These organizations followed Regional Medical Programs and preceded Professional Standards Review Organizations, which were later superseded by Peer Review Organizations.

Experimental Procedures: Any service or product that lacks required scientific evidence of effectiveness in treatment. Also called investigational or unproved procedures.

Expert Witness: A person with specialized education, training, or experience who is able to provide information beyond the knowledge of the average person.

Explanation of Benefits: A statement sent to members explaining how a claim was or was not paid.

Extensive Problem Solving: The type of problem solving consumers use for a completely new or important need, when they put much effort into deciding how to satisfy it.

Extended Care Facility: Long-term care setting that provides skilled, intermediate, or custodial care.

Extension of Benefits: Insurance policy component that allows coverage to continue past termination date for employees not actively in the work force.

External Binary Coded Decimal Interchange Code (EBCDIC): An 8-bit computer code used to represent data. It is the principal code now used in computers and can represent up to 256 distinct characters.

External Constituencies: In a typical health care organization these may be supporters—organizations and people who donate time or money to help the organization function; suppliers—organizations that provide equipment, facilities, and supplies needed by the organization; regulators—licensing bodies, accreditation commissions, and planning and regulatory agencies; and community—the public in general that does not participate in an ongoing exchange relationship with the organization.

External Customer: The traditional customer of an organization's products and services. In health care, the patient and the purchaser (i.e., the employer) are the most notable external customers.

Extraordinary Care: Utilization of advanced technology in medical treatment to keep a patient alive. Examples: kidney dialysis or mechanical ventilation. Medicines, treatments, and procedures that offer no significant health improvement or that cannot be administered without excessive pain.

Extra-Percentage Tables Method: In this method for rating substandard risks, each substandard class is charged a premium that is a certain percentage over the standard premium rate.

Extrinsic Value: Valuable for the external results it produces; a means to an end. See *intrinsic value*.

F

Face Value: The amount payable at maturity to the holder of a bond or note. Also known as *par value* or *maturity value*.

Facilitators: Firms that provide one or more marketing functions other than buying or selling.

FACPE: Fellow of the American College of Physician Executives.

Fact Finder: The person or group of persons in a judicial or administrative proceeding that has the responsibility of determining the facts relevant to decide a controversy. For example, the judge in a nonjury trial, a jury, a hearing officer, or a hearing body.

Factor: A variable that shows the relation of some other variable to the item being forecast; an organization that will purchase the accounts receivable of another entity at a discounted price.

Factor Method: An approach used to forecast sales by finding a relationship between the company's sales and some other factor (or factors).

Faculty Practice Plan: A group practice centered around a teaching program. The plan may be one group encompassing all the physicians providing services to patients at the academic health center or it may be a multispecialty group of specialists.

Fad: An idea that is fashionable only to certain groups who are so fickle that a fad is even more short-lived than a regular fashion.

FAH: Federation of American Hospitals.

Family Brand: A brand name that is used for several products offered by the same company.

FASC: Freestanding ambulatory surgical center.

Favorable Selection: Selection of enrollees who are, on the average, healthier.

Favored Nation Pricing: A contract between a provider and a payer that states that the provider will always match the best discount offered to anyone else.

Favored Nation Discount: An agreement that a provider will automatically provide the payer with the best discount available for services.

FCC: Federal Communications Commission.

FDA: Food and Drug Administration.

Federal Employees Health Benefits Program (FEHBP): Health benefits program administered solely for federal employees.

Federal Fair Packaging and Labeling Act: A 1966 law requiring that consumer goods be clearly labeled in easy-to-understand terms.

Federal Qualification: The Health Maintenance Organization Act of 1973 urged creation of HMOs. Those HMOs that voluntarily opt to comply with regulatory requirements more stringent than the laws in their states are eligible to receive federal grants and loans. The act also required large employers to offer HMO plans to employees if requested by a local HMO.

Federal Trade Commission (FTC): Federal government agency that polices antimonopoly laws and fair business practices.

Federally Qualified HMO: A managed care organization that meets all of the standards established under the federal Health Maintenance Organization Act and thus is eligible for federal funds, Medicare contracting, etc.

Fee for Service: Any payment system in which a provider receives a fee for each unit of good or service provided.

Fee Schedule: A listing of the maximum allowable fees that a health plan pays for particular services, based on CPT billing codes. Also called fee maximums or fee allowance schedule.

Fee Survey: A list of fees charged for specific procedures for comparison in a community.

Feedback: Information from elements of the distribution channel or from consumers that tells an organization's managers about the performance of each marketing program; formal or informal signals sent by the decoder of a message to the encoder.

FEHBP: See Federal Employees Health Benefits Program.

FFS: Fee for service.

FICA: Federal Insurance Contributions Act.

Fiduciary Relationship: In its strictest sense, a status wherein one manages monetary affairs for another and is therefore obligated to act in absolute good faith with regard to those affairs. This same degree of duty has been imposed on others, including, in some jurisdictions, a physician with regard to the safekeeping of information obtained concerning a patient.

Field: A single piece of information, the smallest unit manipulated by a database management system. Also, the series of positions on the computer monitor occupied by the information—for instance, an address.

FIFO (First In, First Out): In inventory management, a method by which the value of the ending inventory is determined from the cost of the most recent purchases and the inventory-related cost of goods or services sold is determined from the cost of the oldest purchases, including the cost of the beginning inventory.

File: A repository of computer data (e.g., a word processing document) or of program instruction (e.g., winword.exe).

Finance: (1) to supply funds for any particular purpose; (2) to supply funds to an organization through the sale of equity or the incurrence of debt; (3) the short term for managerial finance.

Financial Accounting: That branch of accounting that focuses on recording and reporting the past activities of an organization, including the construction of financial statements, in accordance with Generally Accepted Accounting Principles (GAAP).

Financial Accounting Standards Board: Private sector organization in charge of establishing standards of financial accounting and reporting. See *GAAP*.

Financial Accounting Statements: Any of several documents—balance sheet, income statement, statement of retained earnings, statement of cash flows—that describe the financial condition of an entity.

Financial Asset: Any asset that is not a fixed asset See *intangible asset*.

Financial Incentives: Rewards for physicians who practice in a cost-effective manner.

Financial Lease: See *capital lease*.

Financial Ratios: Ratios of various items taken from financial statements. Financial ratios can generally be divided into four categories: liquidity ratios, operating ratios, debt ratios, and profitability ratios. The purpose of these ratios is to provide detailed evidence on an entity's financial soundness or lack of it.

Financial Reserves: Funds managed care companies set aside to cover financial insolvency.

Financial Viability: The likelihood that an entity is organized and operated such that it can survive as an ongoing enterprise indefinitely.

First-Dollar Coverage: A policy that covers all of a patient's medical expenses, with little or no coinsurance and deductibles.

Fiscal Intermediary: An organization that operates as a channel for payment to providers by third-party payers. The intermediary receives claims for payment from providers and makes payments it determines are covered under law or under a contract between the provider and the third party.

Fiscal Year: A period of 12 consecutive months that is designated by an organization as the reporting period for its financial accounting.

Fishbone Chart: A depiction of the relationships between an outcome or effect and its contributors or causes. A visual aid that helps organize cause-and-effect relationships for "things gone wrong."

Five-Stage Model: An earlier quality management problem-solving model developed by the Joint Commission on Accreditation of Healthcare Organizations (JCAHO), involving identification of priorities, verification of key issues, determination of the improvement focus, implementation of improvement actions, and evaluation of the impact of actions.

Fixed Assets: Equipment, land, buildings, and other physical assets that are not normally moved, and are typically used or consumed in the operation of an organization over periods in excess of one year; also referred to as *real* or *tangible assets.*

Fixed Budget: A financial plan in which the amounts specified do not vary with volume or the level of activity. Also called a *"static budget."*

Fixed Cost: A cost that does not vary with volume or frequency in the production of a good or service during a specified period.

Fixed-Cost Contribution Per Unit: The selling price per unit minus the variable cost per unit.

Fixed-Price Package: A benefits package in which the cost for each procedure or service is preset.

Flat Extra Premium Method: Method for rating risk that is considered constant.

Flexible Benefits Plan: See *cafeteria plan.*

Flexible Budget: A financial plan in which the amounts specified vary over a range of activity levels.

Flexible-Price Policy: Policy of offering the same product and quantities to different customers at different prices.

Flex Plan: See *cafeteria plan.*

Flighting Strategy: A media scheduling strategy in which there is heavy advertising during some parts of the campaign and no advertising in between.

Float: Checks that have been credited to the depositor's account but have not yet been debited to the drawer's account. A technique for taking advantage of normal delays in checking transactions in order to secure a financial advantage.

Floppy Disk: A flexible disk of oxide-coated mylar used for the storage of data. Most common sizes are 5-1/4" and 3-1/2". The disk is inserted in the computer drive for data manipulation and processing.

Flow Chart: A diagram of a process, showing each step of the process and how it relates to other steps.

Flowsheet: Tabular presentation of information in a format that permits display of variables that change with time. Also, the software that permits manipulation of the information.

Fluctuating Markets: Situation in which demand for services or exchanges occurs at times the organization isn't prepared to handle it or in which demand varies widely compared to the capacity of the organization to respond.

FMG: Foreign medical graduate.

Focus Group Interview: An interview of 6 to 10 people in an informal group setting with a professionally trained moderator in order to determine their views on some narrow subject, such as a proposed marketing campaign or elements of such a campaign.

Font: A complete set of characters in a particular typeface style and size.

Forecasting: Statistical estimates of what a market segment might buy and how much an industry or firm hopes to sell to a market segment. Techniques available to health organizations fall into three categories: present-centered method—divides current total utilization by the current population to calculate a use rate for a given service (assuming present rates will hold); past-centered method—uses utilization in the past as a basis for forecasting the future; and future-centered method—attempts to predict the future on the basis of speculative analysis (as opposed to quantitative analysis of the past).

Foreseeability: A test used at law to measure the extent of damages for which one may be responsible. Every act will set a series of events in motion that extend to eternity; however, in most jurisdictions, a *tortfeasor* is only responsible for those results that would be reasonably foreseeable. For example, it is reasonably foreseeable that a result of negligent surgery will be the patient's pain and suffering.

Forgone Benefit: In cost accounting, a value that is not achieved because of a decision to follow a course of action that does not include the involved good or service.

Form 10-K: With forms 10-Q and 8-K, reports disclosing material financial and business information that must be filed periodically by publicly held companies with the Securities and Exchange Commission.

Formulary: List of drugs authorized for use by a hospital, managed care organization, or other provider or payer organization.

Forward Contract: A commitment to buy or to sell a specific asset at a specified future time for a specified price.

Foundation Model: Integrated health care delivery system in which a not-for-profit organization is created and in which all assets of system partners or components are vested.

Franchise Operation: In franchise marketing, a franchisor develops a good marketing strategy, and the retail franchise holders are allowed to carry out the strategy in their own units in return for a fee.

Fraudulent Statement: A misstatement made with the intent to deceive another.

Free Market Model: An economic system in which supply and demand for goods and services, and the accompanying pricing, are established entirely within the marketplace by market participants, all of whom have equal access to information and no one of which can individually control any general characteristic of the market.

Freedom of Information Act: Enacted by Congress in 1966, the act requires federal agencies to make certain information available to the public. Medical records are exempt.

Frequency: The average number of times that the average prospect will be exposed to a specific advertisement in a specified period.

Freestanding Emergency Medical Service Center: See *emergicenter*.

Freestanding Outpatient Surgical Center: See *surgicenter*.

Fringe Benefit: Any benefit of employment, such as vacations or health plans, that are separate from and in addition to cash wages or salary.

FSMB: Federation of State Medical Boards.

FTC: Federal Trade Commission

FTE: Full-time equivalent.

Full Capitation: A financial incentive, usually for groups or individual physicians, in which a specific amount of money is allotted to cover all medical services. The HMO reimburses hospitals and deducts the amount from the money allotted physicians. Physicians receive any funds that remain from the capitation pool after claims are paid.

Full Cost: The final cost of each unit of output of an organizational division or cost center to which all indirect costs have been allocated so that all costs, direct and indirect, controllable and noncontrollable, are included; the out part of cost accounting, sometimes called "fully allocated cost."

Full-Cost Approach: Technique in which all functional costs are allocated to products, customers, or other categories.

Full-Line Pricing: Process of setting prices for a whole line of products.

Full Payout Lease: See *capital lease*.

Full-Time Equivalent (FTE): The work time of one or more employees that adds to approximately 2,080 hours per year. In calculating full-time equivalents, a full-time employee is automatically designated as an FTE. The hours of all other employees are added and the result divided by 2,080 to determine the number of additional FTEs.

Functional Accounts: Categories of costs that show the purpose for which the expenditures are made.

Functional Discounts: Reductions from a list price given by a seller to buyers who either give up some marketing function or provide it themselves.

Functional Integration: The extent to which key support functions and activities, such as finance, human resources, strategic planning, information management, marketing, and quality assurance/improvement, are coordinated across units.

Functional Status: The ability of an individual to function physically, socially, mentally, and in the roles to which he or she is accustomed.

Fund: An asset or group of assets set aside for a specific purpose.

Fund Accounting: A method of accounting used by government and other nonprofit organizations in which the organization is viewed as a collection of funds.

Fund Balance: The excess in a fund of assets over liabilities and reserves. The not-for-profit equivalent of stockholders' or partners' equity or net worth.

Fungible: Interchangeable, substitutable, swappable, without change in substance or value; dollar bills are "fungible," as are the shares of common stock of an organization.

Future Damages: That loss or injury expected to occur in the future for which the law allows recovery. In most jurisdictions, with the exception of noneconomic damages such as future pain and suffering, the amount awarded is reduced to its present money value.

Futures Contract: See *forward contract.*

Future Value: The value at a future time of expected future cash flows or of a present value using an appropriate compounding factor known as the discount rate.

Futurism: The study of current and anticipated events to determine likely scenarios for the future.

Futurist: A person who subscribes to the precepts of futurism and builds scenarios for the future.

G

GAAP: Generally Accepted Accounting Principles as defined by the Financial Accounting Standards Board (FASB).

Gain: An excess of revenues over expenses for a single transaction; an increase in value of an asset.

Gatekeeper: Manager of overall patient care, usually a primary care physician. Gatekeeping is the process by which referral for specialized evaluation or treatment is managed, usually by a primary care provider. Can also mean the responsibility of the primary care provider to determine the appropriateness of a patient referral to a specialist for a complicated testing procedure or an alternative treatment. Also, the act of financially limiting a patient's access to specialized services because the primary care physician can perform services at a lower cost. A predominant feature of most HMOs.

Gateway: A connection between two separate and distinct networks that allows transfer of data between them.

GDP: See *gross domestic product*.

Gender identity: A person's concept of himself as being male and masculine or female and feminine, or ambivalent, usually based on physical characteristics, parental attitudes and expectations, and psychological and social pressures to which the individual is subjected. It is the private experience of gender role.

General Damages: Those compensatory damages that one would reasonably expect to result from an act. For example, pain and suffering and disfigurement could all reasonably be expected to result from unnecessary surgery. General damages are distinguishable from special damages, which do not necessarily result from such an act. See *consequential damages*.

General Fund: Assets and liabilities of a nonprofit organization that are not designated for specific purposes; the primary operating account of a government organization.

General Journal: The formal record of transactions made in chronological order as the transactions occur.

General Ledger: The formal record of all the transactions in each account used by an organization. At any given time, the debits and credits for an account are in balance.

Generally Accepted Accounting Principles: See *GAAP*.

General Partnership: Participation in a partnership arrangement such that individual partners are each personally liable for all debts of the organization.

Generic Market: A market whose buying segments have broadly similar needs and whose sellers offer various and often diverse ways of satisfying those needs.

Generic Products: Products that have no brand other than identification of their contents and the manufacturer or middleman.

Generic Substitution: Supplying a generic product even when another product is prescribed by a physician.

Gene Splicing: The technique used when recombinant DNA is produced and made to function within an organism. Also called genetic engineering.

Genetic Counseling: A method used to familiarize, educate and advise individuals of inherited diseases passed on from parents to offspring and a means of dealing with the psychological difficulties associated with it.

Genetic Engineering: See *gene splicing*.

Genetics: Area of biology dealing with heredity and the role of genes in the inherited characteristics of an individual or organism.

Geographic Adjustment Factor (GAF): A factor used in third-party payment systems (e.g., Medicare) to adjust for geographic differences in the costs providers pay for resources.

Geographic Service Points: Hospitals and physicians located conveniently to enrollees' places of employment and homes.

GHAA: Group Health Association of America.

Global Budget: Prospective caps on health care spending aimed at curtailing growth of the health care delivery system.

Global Fee: A variation of fee for service, one fee that covers all services rendered during an episode of care.

GMENAC: Graduate Medical Education National Advisory Committee.

GNP: See *gross national product*.

Goal: An objective of the organization that is made specific with respect to magnitude, time, and responsibility.

Goal Programming: A mathematical technique for allocating resources among competing uses on the basis of qualitative criteria.

Good Distribution of Risk: The presence in a group of sufficient healthy insured to offset the claims of a few unhealthy ones.

Good Samaritan Laws: Statutes enacted in all states that, although varied in their detail, generally provide some form of immunity to those who, without a duty to act, nevertheless render aid in an emergency.

Goodwill: In accounting, the difference between the fair market value of the assets of a purchased organization or operating unit and their value as recorded by financial accounting.

Governing Body: The individuals, group, or agency that has ultimate responsibility for an organization's policies, for its management and planning, and for the quality of the products and services it offers.

Grace Period: The length of time after a premium is due but unpaid for which the policy and all its riders remain in effect.

Graphic User Interface (GUI): Computer control system that allows the user to command the computer by "pointing and clicking," using a mouse, at icons or pictures representing applications or files in computer memory.

Graphic: A picture or illustration generated by a computer and displayed on screen, paper, or film. Requires special computers and computer hardware.

Gray Scale: A computer scheme for representing intensity within a black-and-white image. Involves use of varying bits per graphics pixel.

Grievance Procedures: A written plan based on state and federal regulations that specifies the time limit for member grievances, identifies the grievance reviewer, and spells out a member's recourse.

Gross: A statistic not yet subjected to any reductions or adjustments.

Gross Domestic Product (GDP): The market value of all goods and services produced or sold within a country's borders for any given period.

Gross Margin (Gross Profit): The money left after covering the cost of producing a product or service to cover the expenses of selling the product or service and operating the business.

Gross National Product (GNP): The market value of all goods and services produced or sold in or by a country for any given period, i.e., it includes the effects of imports and exports, which are not part of GDP.

Gross Negligence: A degree of negligence more aggravated than simply failing to conduct oneself with due regard to the duty owed to others. Although some courts have merged the concept of gross negligence into that of willful, wanton, and reckless acts, others hold that the latter is a higher degree of negligence than gross negligence, in that it evidences an express or implied intent to harm.

Gross Premium: The net premium plus a loading factor.

Gross Sales: The total amount charged to all customers during some period.

Group: Body of subscribers of a health plan. Also body of physicians organized to collectively provide and bill for health care services.

Group Contract: An agreement between an HMO and a group of subscribers that specifies rates, performance covenants, relationships among parties, schedule of benefits, and other conditions.

Group Insurance: Coverage for several persons under one contract, called a master contract.

Group-Model HMO: An HMO that contracts with a medical group for provision of health care. A form of closed-panel health plan.

Group Practice Model: A type of HMO in which physicians share the use of a central HMO facility. See *individual practice association*.

Group Practice without Walls: The sharing of administrative costs by physicians in a corporate structure, with the physicians maintaining separate practices and revenue streams.

GSA: General Services Administration.

Guaranteed Renewable Policy: An individual health insurance policy that the insurer agrees to continue until the insured reaches a specified age if premium payments, which the insurer may change, are made on the due date.

Guaranty Funds: Programs established by a state to financially cover an HMO's liabilities if it should become insolvent.

Guardian Ad Litem: An individual charged by a court with the authority and duty to represent the interests of a minor or an incompetent adult in a legal action.

H

Habeas Corpus: The procedure to challenge the legality of detention or custody.

Hard Disk: Hardware for auxiliary storage of large amounts of data. May be a separate device or be located within the computer.

Hard Lock-in: Contract provision in which enrollees are locked into a specific plan and cannot opt out to another.

Hardware: The physical components of a computer, such as central processing unit, keyboard, monitor, printer, modem, and data storage devices.

Harvard Test: Widely accepted criteria for determining brain death that were formulated in 1960. Included are unreceptivity and unresponsiveness, lack of movement or breathing, lack of reflexes, and flat electroencephalogram.

HCFA: Health Care Financing Administration.

HCFA 1500: Form used by the Health Care Financing Administration for billing by providers.

HCFA Common Procedural Coding System (HCPCS): Coding system used by Medicare carriers that includes CPT codes, national codes developed by HCFA, and codes developed by local Medicare carriers.

HCFA Mortality Data: See *mortality data*.

Health Care Financing Administration: Federal agency responsible for administering the Medicare program and for monitoring the states' administration of the Medicaid program.

Health Care Quality Improvement Act of 1986: A federal law that established the National Practitioner Data Bank and provided limited relief from antitrust litigation for organizations and individuals involved in the peer review process.

Health Care Reform: Innovation and improvement in the health care system by reappraisal, amendment of services, and removal of faults and abuses in providing and distributing services to patients.

Health Costs: The actual funds spent by providers on the health care of patients. See *health expenditures*.

Health Economics: The study of the financing, production, and consumption of health care services.

Health Employer Data and Information Set (HEDIS): Performance measures developed by the National Committee on Quality Assurance to assist health care buyers to judge and compare health plans.

Health Expenditures: The actual funds paid to providers for the health care of patients. See *health costs*.

Health Insurance: Insurance covering losses from sickness or injury. The two main types of health insurance are medical expense coverage and disability income coverage.

Health Insurance Portability and Accountability Act of 1996 (Kennedy-Kassenbaum Bill): This legislation ensures that individuals who leave (or lose) their jobs can obtain some type of health insurance coverage, even if they or someone in their immediate family has serious illness, injury, or pregnancy. The law specifically limited insurers' ability to impose preexisting condition clauses on insureds.

Health Law: The application of the principles of law and justice to health and medicine.

Health Maintenance Organization (HMO): An arrangement in which one or more selected care providers agree to provide a defined set of health care/medical care services to selected populations (e.g., employee groups) for a fixed dollar amount per covered life (member) for a specified period. The providers assume the risk of intensity of services beyond that forecast. Covered persons are typically restricted to specific panels of providers that may be fairly small (staff-model HMOs) or fairly large (IPA-model HMOs), and may also be responsible for small copayments.

Health Maintenance Organization Regulatory Agency: State agency with the power to grant or rescind an HMO's ability to do business, to license solicitors, and to regulate itself. In most states, that agency is the insurance department.

Health Plan Purchasing Cooperative (HPPC): Under managed competition, individuals could buy coverage from Accountable Health Plans through the HPPC.

Health Policy: Decisions, usually developed by government policy makers, for determining present and future objectives of the health care system.

Health Resources: The elements in the universe of individuals, organizations, products, and services that are available to meet the health care needs of a particular individual.

Health Status: The level of health of an individual as measured at a given time.

Healthcare Forum Commitment to Quality Award: An annual award presented to health care organizations and individuals who demonstrate commitment to the provision of high-quality services to patients.

Heavy Half: A small group of consumers who purchase a share of a product disproportionate to its size. See *Pareto Principle* and *Eighty-Twenty (80/20) Rule*.

HEDIS: See *Health Employer Data and Information Set*.

Hedonism: The doctrine that pleasure or happiness is everything.

HEW: Department of Health, Education, and Welfare.

HFMA: Healthcare Financial Management Association.

HHA: Home Health Agency.

HHS: Department of Health and Human Services.

HIAA: Health Insurance Association of America.

Hierarchy of Effects: The purpose of communication and promotion efforts is to move prospective customers progressively from unawareness to awareness, to understanding/familiarity, to interest, to decision, to utilization, to satisfaction, to repeated/regular use, to recommendation.

Hill-Burton Act: Federal legislation enacted in 1946 that provided subsidies for hospital building projects, largely in rural areas.

HIMA: Health Industries Manufacturers Association.

HIMSS: Hospital Information Management Systems Society.

HIS: Hospital information system, health information system.

HISSG: Hospital information system sharing group.

Histogram: A pictorial or graphic summary of a set of data to highlight patterns.

Historical Cost: Another term for acquisition, original, or sunk cost.

HMO: See *health maintenance organization*.

HMO Act of 1973: Federal law that requires employers with more than 24 employees to offer a federally qualified HMO as an alternative to indemnity coverage.

HIMSS: Hospital Information Management Systems Society.

Hold Harmless Clause: A contractual agreement whereby the parties involved will not hold one another liable under specified conditions, for instance malpractice or corporate malfeasance when one party is already found to be liable. Written into contracts between HMOs and providers, the clause protects members from HMO insolvency because it does not allow providers to bill members for sums owed to the HMO.

Holding: The court's decision on the specific question under consideration in a hearing. The holding has precedential significance. Sometimes the term is used more broadly to indicate any ruling of the court.

Holding Company: An organization that produces no goods or services itself but has controlling interest (more than 50 percent) in one or more companies. The holding company also supervises the management of the held companies.

Home Care: Health care services provided in the patient's residence.

Home-Field Advantage: Locating an HMO facility near where members live and work.

Homogeneous Shopping Products: Products the customer sees as the same and wants at the lowest price.

Horizontal Agreement: An agreement between or among direct competitors.

Horizontal Conflict: Conflict that occurs between members at the same level of the distribution channel.

Horizontal Integration: Coordination of activities across operating units that are at the same stage in the process of delivering services, such as acute hospital care.

Hospice: Facility for providing supportive health care services to the terminally ill.

Hospital Confinement Policy: A policy that provides a predetermined flat daily rate for hospitalization, regardless of length of stay.

Hospital Indemnity Policy: See *hospital confinement policy*.

Hospital Payment System: The main payment systems used by managed care companies are discounted charges, per diems, per stay, and capitation.

Hospital-Surgical Expense Policy: A policy that covers expenses related directly to hospitalization, surgery, and associated medical procedures incurred for treatment of an illness or injury.

HSMHA: Health Services and Mental Health Administration.

Hub and Spoke Network: A managed care provider network in which hospitals and physicians send patients to various levels of care.

Human Relations: Human problems that arise as a result of interpersonal or organizational relations, or a course or program designed to improve working conditions or communication among people.

Human Rights: A term related to actively promoting the needs and welfare of people according to standards of what society has determined to be just, legal, and morally good. Also, the doctrine that espouses the belief that all humans are entitled to basic freedoms, including freedom of speech and freedom to choose.

Humanitarianism: Promotion of human welfare and social reform.

Humulin: A genetically designed form of human insulin. Recombines selected clone genes to create a hormone that can be used to treat and control diabetes mellitus.

Hurdle Rate: Minimally acceptable rate of return for an investment; a rate that a proposal's internal rate of return must exceed for the proposal to be economically acceptable.

Hybrid-Model HMO: An HMO model that combines the features of two or more other HMO models.

Hypothesis: A tentative assumption about the relationship between two or more things or about what will happen in the future that is then used to test the validity of the relationship or of the prediction.

I

Iatrogenic: A disease or injury introduced to a patient by a provider.

ICD-9-CM: A detailed disease and condition classification system that is the basis for most hospital and provider billing procedures.

Iceberg Principle: The tendency for much good information to be hidden in summary data.

Icon: An on-screen graphic that may be used to access programs, data files, commands, or other stored or computer-embedded information.

Ideal Market Exposure: Availability of a product widely enough to satisfy target customers' needs but not exceed them.

IHCDS: Integrated health care delivery system.

Illness Pattern: Studying the health of a specific population and noting similarities.

Illness Perils: See *accident perils*.

Immediate Write-Off: In accounting, the recognition of the cost of a fixed asset in the period in which it is acquired.

Impact Printer: A data output device that imprints through contact of raised type against paper, using ink or ribbon as the transfer medium.

Impact Report: A report prepared by an HMO that documents cost and utilization.

Impaired Physician: A physician who cannot safely and effectively perform duties because of abuse of drugs or alcohol, a mental disability, emotional problems, or other conditions separate from professional competence.

Impairment Rider: See *exclusion rider*.

Impairment Waiver: See *exclusion rider*.

Impeachment: An attempt to discredit the testimony of a witness. Impeachment is usually accomplished by presenting facts that either contradict the testimony or suggest that the witness is generally not worthy of belief.

Implementation: Putting marketing plans into operation.

Implicit Approach: In determinations of the appropriateness of diagnosis, treatment, or procedures, the use of a clinician's judgment rather than a formal analytical process.

Implied Consent: Assumed approval for a course of medical treatment or for a procedure.

Impressions: The total number of exposures to a specific advertisement in a specified period.

Improvement Knowledge: System variation, psychology, and theory of knowledge leading to continual improvement of health care.

Impulse Products: Products that are bought quickly as unplanned purchases because of a strongly felt need.

Incentives: Monetary or other encouragements offered to clinicians to entice them to practice medicine in specific, usually more cost-effective, ways.

Income: In accounting, the difference between revenues and expenses for a given period.

Income from Operations: The net results of sales of an organization's goods and services.

Income Statement: A financial accounting statement that summarizes expenses, revenues, gains, and losses for an organization in any given period. The income statement may also show earnings per share, changes in retained earnings, and other derivative data for the period. It is sometimes called a *statement of revenues and expenses*.

Income Tax: An annual levy by local, state, or federal governments on the net income of an individual or organization.

Incremental Analysis: An assessment of a proposed course of action that focuses exclusively on items that will be altered by the proposal if it is adopted. Incremental analysis includes consideration of opportunity costs and forgone benefits, and excludes all consideration of reallocations of preexisting indirect costs or overheads.

Incremental Cost: Costs that will be incurred only if an activity is undertaken.

Incurred But Not Reported (IBNR): Money accrued by a plan for medical expenses that it is as yet unaware of.

Indemnity: A contract or assurance by which one person agrees to secure another against anticipated loss. The legal duty to reimburse another who has discharged a liability owed by oneself. Such a duty can be created by contract between the parties, as where a person agrees to assume responsibility for the acts of another. It can also, in many jurisdictions, be created by rule of law, as where one's obligation to pay is not due to his or her own active negligence, but rather to a vicarious responsibility for another whose act caused the liability. For example, a physician who was not actively negligent may be held liable for the act of an employee who was negligent. The physician may then seek indemnity or total reimbursement from the employee for the sums the physician was obligated to pay.

Indemnity Carrier: Insurer that offers coverage under a framework of negotiated fee schedules and conditions.

Indemnity Insurance: Coverage paying cash benefits after a covered loss in accordance with a framework of fee schedules.

Indemnity Opt-Out Product: Enrollees' option of changing to HMO coverage.

Indenture: See *bond indenture*.

Independent Auditor: A person or organization from outside an organization who checks the organization's financial records for accuracy and completeness and who formally assures users of the organization's statements that the information meets accepted standards for financial reporting.

Independent Practice Association (IPA): An organization that contracts with a managed care plan to deliver services in return for a specific capitation rate. The IPA then contracts with individual providers to provide the services on a capitation or fee-for-service basis.

Indexing: Techniques for tying amounts fixed in law or contracts to the effects of inflation. The fixed amounts change in response to changes in the CPI or other accepted indexes.

Indictment: A formal written accusation, which is presented to a grand jury, charging a person with criminal conduct.

Indirect Advertising: Competitive advertising that points out product advantages in order to affect future buying decisions.

Indirect Costs: Costs that are not directly related to particular goods, services, or activities, such as overhead costs, that, while necessary, are not specific to the output or activity.

Indirect Standardization: In severity indexing methods, the use of outcomes data from the general population in conjunction with provider-specific outcomes data to determine risk-adjustment factors.

Individual Brands: Use of separate brand names for each product or product line.

Individual Practice Association: See *independent practice association*.

Individual Product: A particular product within a product line.

Industrial Marketing: The process of anticipating, discovering, and designing product and service specifications that will satisfy the requirements of industrial customers.

Inelastic Demand: Situation in which, although the quantity demanded increases if the price is decreased, it will not stretch enough to avoid a decrease in total revenue.

Inelastic Supply: Situation in which the quantity supplied does not stretch much (if at all) if the price is raised.

Inert Market: Similar to situation in the negative exchange in that no exchanges take place. The difference is that, in the inert market, potential constituents are simply indifferent.

Infection Control: The individuals, processes, and protocols that are used to ensure that nosocomial infections are minimized or eliminated.

Inflation: A condition of generally rising prices for goods and services.

Inflow: See *receipt*.

Influence: Power to sway or affect on the basis of ability, position, prestige, wealth, etc.

Informatics: The whole of information technology and its applications.

Information Science: The study of the creation, use, and communication of information.

Information Sharing: Comparison of physician practice patterns and/or performance and cost information provided by HMOs and hospitals for sharing with consumers.

Information System: Equipment and procedures used for the collection, recording, processing, storage, retrieval, and display of information.

Information Theory: The mathematical formulations that explain the communication of information.

Informed Consent: Autonomous, voluntary decisions agreeing to medical procedures made by people deemed mentally competent. Oral or written consent is granted by a patient after a physician has disclosed information pertinent to making the decision. The amount of necessary information to be imparted to a patient will vary according to the jurisdiction. It generally includes the nature of the illness, the nature of the proposed therapy, reasonable alternative therapies, the likelihood of obtaining a desired result, and the substantial risks of the proposed therapy and of failing to undergo therapy. See *negligence theory.*

Informed Refusal: Rejection of treatment by a patient or his or her representatives after provision of full information on the treatment's benefits and risks. See *refusal.*

Initial Public Offering (IPO): The first offering of a security.

Initiator: In the exchange process, the person who first recognizes an unsatisfied want or need.

Injunction: Judicial prohibition requiring a party to refrain from doing or continuing to do some specific activity or act. A preliminary injunction is awarded prior to a trial on the merits of a case and is only temporary. It may be made permanent following the trial.

In Loco Parentis: "In place of parents"; a legal doctrine that allows a "stand-in" to exercise the legal rights, duties, and responsibilities a parent possesses toward a child.

Innovation: The development and spread of new ideas and products.

Inpatient: Person admitted to a hospital for at least 24 hours of care under the supervision of a physician.

Input Device: Hardware, such as a keyboard, a mouse, or a light pen, used to enter data into a computer.

Insider: A person or organization that has access to nonpublic information surrounding the financial condition of an organization or about its financial planning.

Insolvency: Inability to pay debts at the time specified.

Inspection Receipt: A document that states that an insurance policy has not been "delivered" even though it has been placed in the hands of the insured. Insurance is normally not in effect under this receipt.

Inspection Report: The results of an insurer's investigation into the suitability of an applicant for insurance.

Installation: All activities from the purchase of a group policy through issuance of the policy and individual certificates. Also, the process by which software programs are stored on a computer.

Institutional Advertising: Advertising that tries to promote an organization's image, reputation, or ideas rather than a specific product.

Institutional Ethics Committee: An interdisciplinary group that addresses ethical concerns and questions, especially those of patient care. The group facilitates clinical decision-making, provides a venue for ethical discussions, and educates staff on ethical matters. The committee can also be charged with establishment of ethical guidelines and policies. See *ethics committee*.

Institutional Liability: See *corporate liability*.

Instruction: Coding that defines an operation that is requested of a computer.

Insured: The person whose health care is insured under the policy.

Insured Product Option (IPO): Preferred provider organization option offered by an insurer in addition to traditional indemnity products.

Insurer: The party in the policy who agrees to pay a benefit when specified losses occur.

Intangible Asset: In accounting, a nonphysical, noncurrent asset, such as a copyright, a patent, a trademark, or goodwill; more generally, any financial asset, including nonphysical accrued assets, often referred to collectively as "intangibles."

Integrated Health Care Delivery System (IHCOS): A health care system that combines physicians, hospitals, and other medical services with a health plan to provide the complete spectrum of medical care for its customers. In a fully integrated system, the three key elements—physicians, hospitals, and health plan membership—are in balance in terms of matching medical resources with the needs of purchasers and patients.

Intelligent Terminal: An input/output device in which computer processing components are built into the terminal.

Intensity: A measure of the level of use of resources by an organization in the production of a good or provision of a service, per unit of output.

Intensive Distribution: Selling a product through all responsible and suitable wholesalers or retailers who will stock and/or sell the product.

Interest: The cost of purchasing or using money.

Interest Rate: The cost of purchasing or using money, expressed as a percentage of the amount purchased or used per period of time, usually one year.

Interest Rate Risk: The potential gain or loss in the market value of a capital claim, especially a debt claim, that results from volatility in market rates of interest.

Interface: The physical (connector or keyboard) or logical (software) link between the computer and a user or peripheral device (printer, modem, etc.).

Internal Audit: The use of organizational employees to check the effectiveness of an organization's financial control procedures.

Internal Constituencies: Likely to be included among a health organization's internal constituents are: boards of trustees, committees, etc. that serve policy making, advisory, and other ongoing functions; employees, who provide the direct services of the organization and are linked in a formal employee/employer relationship; physicians, who refer patients, supervise the care of such patients, and serve as agents of the organization but are not employees; and volunteers and members of auxiliaries who perform direct services but receive no payment/financial benefit.

Internal Customer: An employee, department, division, or other subsection of an organization that consumes the products or services of other employees, departments, divisions, or subsections of the organization.

Internal Rate of Return: A single discount rate that, when used to discount a stream of cash flows, including the initial cash outlay, results in a net present value of zero.

International Classification of Diseases, Ninth Revision, Clinical: See *ICD-9-CM*.

International Code of Medical Ethics: A professional code established in 1949 that states, "A doctor shall preserve absolute secrecy on all he knows about his patient because of the confidence entrusted to him."

Internet: International computer communications system and protocols that link computers and computer networks.

Interpreter: An internal computer translator that converts source language into machine language.

Interrogatory: Questions sent from one party in a lawsuit to another party in the suit that are designed to elicit information necessary to prepare a case. They are commonly used in the discovery process prior to trial and are usually sent in written form, requiring a written answer under oath.

Intervening Cause: An independent act that occurs between the time of the original negligence or malpractice and the time of injury. An intervening cause will absolve the original actor of liability only if the intervening act is totally independent and not reasonably foreseeable by the original actor. For example, if a physician commits a negligent act that will ultimately result in the patient's injury and a different physician commits a later negligent act that triggers the injury, the original physician may still be held liable, as most courts hold the actions of the second physician to have been foreseeable by the first.

Intranet: A computer-based information sharing system within a single organization.

Intrinsic Value: Worth that is self-contained and not dependent on any external factors.

Introductory Price Dealing: Temporary price cuts to speed new products into a market.

Inventory: The amount of goods being stored for later distribution. The balance in any physical asset account, such as materials, or supplies.

Inventory Turnover: A measure of the effectiveness of inventory management; the statistic represents the number of times that inventory is sold in a given period. It is calculated as the cost of goods sold during the period divided by the average value of the inventory during the same period.

Investigational Procedures: See *experimental procedures*.

Investment: In finance, a disbursement for the acquisition of resources (assets) expected to be used, consumed, or sold (liquidated) over a period extending beyond one year.

Investment Bank: A financial institution that plans, underwrites, and distributes new investment securities on behalf of clients issuing the securities.

In Vitro Fertilization: Fertilization of an egg performed outside the body in a laboratory setting with the objective of producing a baby.

Invoice: A document that shows the details of a sales transaction.

IPA: Independent (or Individual) Practice Association; an HMO model in which a number of care providers not otherwise related by ownership form an association to provide prepaid care, establishing contracts among the association members and others that provide for the distribution of capitation (prepaid) monies received by the IPA.

Irrebuttable Presumption: A legal proposition that allows the fact finder (judge or jury) to accept a fact as true if other underlying facts are proven. The presumption becomes irrebuttable when, depending on the jurisdiction, the opposing party is not allowed to offer evidence to contradict the ultimate fact, once the underlying facts have been proven.

Irreversible Coma: A persistent vegetative state from which there is no hope of recovery.

Ishikawa Diagram: See *fishbone chart*.

Issue of Fact: A question regarding the existence of a fact that is generally presented for determination to the fact finder (judge or jury).

Issue of Law: A legal determination, made by a judge alone, requiring that the judge apply legal principles to the facts for a resolution of the matter. This may occur in a summary judgment proceeding where one party accepts, for the purpose of argument, all facts asserted by the opposing party, but claims that, in spite of these facts, he or she is entitled under the law to a judgment in his or her favor. For example, the statute of limitations may mandate a judgment in one's favor in spite of the underlying fact that negligence occurred.

J

JCAHO: Joint Commission on Accreditation of Healthcare Organizations.

Joint and Several Liability: A rule of law that allows one who has suffered loss or injury as a result of the acts of more than one person to collect the entire compensation from any one of the wrongdoers without regard to his or her individual fault or contribution.

Joint Commission on Accreditation of Healthcare Organizations: The most prominent national organization for the accreditation of health care facilities, primarily hospitals.

Joint Tortfeasors: Two or more persons who have acted in concert, each negligently, in producing an injury or loss or whose separate negligent acts, though not in concert, combined to create a single injury or loss. In some jurisdictions, such activity is the basis for the imposition of joint and several liability.

Joint Venture: A business endeavor between two or more parties for a specific purpose, often characterized by mutual control and sharing of the risks and profits of the undertaking.

Journal: In financial management, a place, electronic or paper, where transactions are recorded by accounting as they occur.

Joystick: Electromechanical device that is used to move the computer cursor. Usually used with video games.

Judgment: The conclusion of the court on the claims of the parties as submitted for determination.

Judgment of Moral Obligation: Choice of the action to be performed or avoided in a specific situation, according to standards set by society.

Jurisdiction: The power or authority of a court over the individuals or property in dispute and the subject matter of the dispute.

Jury of Executive Opinion: A practice of forecasting by combining the opinions of experienced executives, perhaps from marketing, production, finance, purchasing, and top management.

Justice: Provision to individuals of equal treatment. How people are treated when their interests compete and are compared against others. See *distributive justice*.

Just-in-Time Delivery: A supplier's practice of reliably getting products to the customer just before they are needed.

Kaizen: A Japanese expression for the achievement of higher and higher levels of performance by doing things better and setting increasingly higher standards.

Karen Quinlan: Case that eventually reached the U.S. Supreme Court in which the question was: If there is no hope of returning the patient to a functionally human state, does treatment to prolong life become a circumstance that prolongs death? If so, the act of treatment may be unethical. The patient in question was removed from artificial respiration by the courts at her parents' request and over a hospital's objections. The ethical issues were blurred by the fact that she survived without the respiratory for several years.

Keyboard: Electromechanical alphanumeric device for typing program commands and data for a computer.

Key Field: Coding within a record that uniquely identifies a record within a file.

Key Measures: Factors in the quality of process or service as viewed by the internal or external customer.

Kiting: The practice of taking advantage of the time that elapses between deposit of a check in one bank and its collection from another (*the float*). Also referred to as "playing the float."

Knowledge Base: The database of facts, inferences, and procedures needed for problem solving on a particular subject.

L

Labor: The cost of human resources required to produce goods or services.

Lag Study: A report that lists claims paid out and compares total claims to the amount accrued for expenses each month. It lets planners know if plan reserves are adequate.

Laggards: Persons or organizations that prefer to do things the way they have been done in the past and are very suspicious of new ideas; sometimes called nonadopters. See *adoption curve*.

Laissez-Faire Model: See *free market model*.

LAN: Local area network.

Lapse: Termination of a policy because of nonpayment of premiums.

Lapse Rate: The probability that a policy will lapse by the end of a policy year.

Large-Case Management: Individual management of high cost and/or high risk cases.

Laser: Light amplification by stimulated emission of radiation.

Laser Printer: A nonimpact output device that uses laser technology for transfer of data images to paper.

Late Majority: A group of adopters who are cautious about new ideas. See *adoption curve*.

Law of Diminishing Demand: The principle that, if the price of a product is raised, a smaller quantity will be demanded, and, if the price of a product is lowered, a greater quantity will be demanded.

Law of Large Numbers: A theory of probability that specifies that the greater the number of observations made of an event, the more likely it will be that the observed results will produce the "true" probability of the event's occurring.

LCCME: Liaison Committee on Continuing Medical Education.

LCGME: Liaison Committee on Graduate Medical Education.

LCME: Liaison Committee on Medical Education.

Leader Pricing: The practice of setting very low prices on selected products to get customers into retail stores. See *loss leader*.

Learning Curve: The relationship between the time required to learn new skills and the level of knowledge achieved.

Lease: A contract that specifies the cost (usually in the form of rent) and conditions for the use of an asset by someone (lessee) other than its owner (lessor).

Ledger: A formal book or recording of financial accounts.

Legal Actions Provision: A limit on the period during which a claimant may sue the insurer to collect a disputed claim amount and the specification that no suit may be brought against the insurer until 60 days after a claim is filed.

Length of Stay: A statistical measure of patient turnover for inpatients calculated by dividing the total number of patient days in a period by the total number of discharges in the same period. The number of uninterrupted days a patient spends in a hospital for a single injury or condition. A basic statistic for the determination of hospital utilization.

Lessee: See *lease*.

Lessor: See *lease*.

Letter of Credit: A document issued by a lender to certify that the person named in the letter is entitled to draw funds from the lender up to a specified amount.

Leverage: The use of debt to enhance an organization's ability to acquire assets. Often used as a name for the debt-to-total assets ratio. Referred to as "gearing" in the United Kingdom.

Liability: Legal responsibility for the unexpected results of an individual's or an organization's actions. In the latter case, the organization assumes liability for its employees and contractors. A legal obligation to make payment(s) of specified amount(s) at a specified future time or times.

Libel: Defamation through use of written or printed materials.

Libertarian Theory: Upholding the principles of absolute and unrestricted freedom.

Licensing: Selling the right to use some process, trademark, patent, or other asset for a fee or royalty.

Licensure: Granting by a government entity, usually at the state or a lower level, of the legal right to practice a profession or to operate a business.

Lien: The legal right of one person to satisfy a claim against another person by holding the latter person's property as security or by seizing the property.

Life Expectancy: An actuarially determined statistic that predicts the average age an individual might expect to attain, given his or her current age and, sometimes, life-style characteristics.

Life-Style Analysis: The analysis of a person's day-to-day pattern of living as expressed in that person's activities, interests, and opinions—sometimes referred to as AIOs or psychographics.

LIFO (Last In, First Out): In inventory management, a method by which the value of the ending inventory is determined from the cost of the oldest purchases and the inventory-related cost of goods sold is determined from the cost of the most recent purchases.

Light Pen: Photosensitive device used in conjunction with the monitor and software to provide data and program commands.

Like-Kind Exchange: The exchange by two organizations of similar assets.

Limited Coverage Policy: Medical expense policy that covers only the expenses associated with treatment of a specified disease or diseases.

Limited Liability Corporation: Corporation in which individual stockholders are not liable for the debts of the organization.

Limited Partnership: Status of a partner such that legal obligations for the debts of the partnership may not exceed the partner's actual investment in the partnership, thus protecting such a partner's assets outside of the partnership. A partnership must have at least one general partner having unlimited legal responsibility for debts.

Line Extension: A new variety of a basic product.

Line of Business: The product(s) or service(s) that a company or part of a company offers. Also, a health plan that is set up within a larger organization, generally an insurance company. This designation differentiates it from a freestanding company or one set up as a subsidiary.

Line of Credit: An arrangement with lending institutions for short-term borrowing on demand. A fee is typically charged for the establishment of a line of credit, whether or not the line is actually used. In addition, interest is charged on any actual draw (use) of the line. Generally, all draws are expected to be fully repaid at least once annually.

Liquid Assets: Assets, such as cash that can be used immediately and assets such as marketable securities and current accounts receivable, that can be or are expected to be converted into cash in a short time.

Liquidating Dividend: A return of capital in cash or in kind to equity suppliers; sometimes is used to refer to the final distribution to equity suppliers upon the liquidation of an organization.

Liquidation: The sale of assets. It can refer to a particular asset or to the conversion of all of the assets of an organization to cash at the termination or "winding up" of the organization.

Liquidity: A measure of an organization's ability to gain quick access to the value of its assets.

Liquidity Ratio: Any of a number of financial ratios (e.g., the current ratio, the acid test ratio) that provide some indication of an organization's liquidity.

Literature Search: Use of software program that permits key word scanning of literature databases for articles and books on selected topics.

Living Will: Instructional directives in written form that indicate the author's wishes for medical treatment should he or she become incapacitated and unable to participate in medical decision-making. Natural death acts are pieces of legislation generally enacted to codify living wills and often contain specific examples.

LOA: Leave of absence.

Loading: A charge added to the net premium to cover the operating expenses of the insurer.

Loan Agreement: The legally binding contract that governs the financial relationship between the debtor and the lender.

Local Area Network (LAN): Linked computers and software programs that permit sharing of data and peripheral devices by multiple users in a single site.

Locality Rule: A test used in malpractice law for measuring the required level of care for a patient. It is based on the level of care provided by similar practitioners in the same or a similar community.

Lockbox System: A system in which banks are authorized to collect customer payments directly from post office boxes, record them, and credit them to an organization's account.

Lock-In: HMO condition that care is not covered unless provided or authorized by the HMO. See *hard lock-in*.

Logistics: Transporting and storing goods so as to match target customers' needs with a firm's marketing mix, both within individual firms and along a channel of distribution.

Long-Term: In accounting, an adjective used to refer to liabilities or debt to be repaid at a time or times more than one year hence and to assets expected to be used or maintained for periods in excess of one year; more generally, referring to an open-ended or lengthy period or to the time point at the end of such a period.

Long-Run Target Return Pricing: Pricing technique to cover all costs and achieve an average target return over the long run.

LOS: Length of stay.

Loss: An excess of expenses over revenues for a single transaction, a decrease in the value of an asset.

Loss Leader: Practice of pricing a product below cost to attract customers to other products or services within the company's line.

Loss Rate: The number and timing of losses that will occur in a group during coverage.

Loss Ratio: See *medical loss ratio*.

Lost Chance of Cure: An element of damages. In essence, it allows recovery if a patient's opportunity to be cured of a disease has been reduced because of another's negligence. Some jurisdictions require proof that a cure was probable prior to the negligent act but is no longer probable as a result of the negligence.

Lost Chance of Survival: An element of damages. In essence, it allows recovery if a patient's opportunity to survive a disease has been reduced by another's negligence. Some jurisdictions require proof that survival was probable prior to the negligent act but is no longer probable as a result of the negligence.

Low-Involvement Purchases: Purchases that have little importance or relevance for the customer.

LTC: Long-term care.

M

MAC: Maximum allowable cost.

Machine Language: The basic language of a computer requiring no further translation.

Macro: A single source language statement that, when translated, results in a series of machine-language statements.

Macro-allocation: A form of rationing. The determination of how much should be allocated for resources and what resources should be made available, as opposed to micro-allocation, another form of rationing, in which decisions are made as to who will benefit from the resources.

Macro-Marketing: A social process that directs an economy's flow of goods and services from producers to consumers in a way that effectively matches supply and demand and accomplishes the objectives of society.

Magnetic Tape: A data storage device, usually in a cassette.

Magnuson-Moss Act: A 1975 federal law requiring that producers provide a clearly written warranty if they choose to offer any warranty.

Mainframe: Large computers with large amounts of storage capacity and the ability to process large amounts of data very quickly.

Major Diagnostic Category: Within the DRG framework, a broad classification of diagnoses grouped by body system.

Major Medical Policy: Medical expense policy that provides broad coverage for both hospital and outpatient expenses. Policies generally have few limitations, high maximum benefits, and high deductibles.

Malcolm Baldrige National Quality Award: Administered by the U.S. Department of Commerce and named for a past Secretary of Commerce, this prestigious award goes annually to companies that meet the rigorous standards of the program for the manufacture and sale of products and services.

Malpractice: A cause of action for which damages are allowed, characterized by the failure of a professional to adhere to the applicable standards of his or her profession in the manner in which he or she renders services.

MAM: Master's degree in administrative medicine.

Managed Care Organization (MCO): A health care delivery system that offers, finances, and delivers medical care at a fixed premium to a defined population.

Managed Care: A system of health care delivery that influences utilization of services, costs of services, and measurement of performance. Usually stresses preventive care and is often associated with an HMO.

Managed Competition: A health care system whereby employees receive a fixed sum from their employer and choose their own health care plan. If the plans they choose cost more than the allotted sum, employees pay the difference. There is a tax incentive for employees to select lower priced options because they can only deduct the amount of the lowest cost option. Under this system, there are no provisions to set premiums that cover individual patient or specific patient population risk.

Managed Health Care: A wide variety of systems of health care delivery and financing that attempt to manage the cost and quality of care as well as access to that care.

Management Contracting: Marketing arrangement in which the seller provides only management skills; others own production and distribution facilities.

Management Information Systems: Equipment and procedures used for the collection, recording, processing, storage, retrieval, and display of information relevant to an organization.

Management Services Organization (MSO): A legal entity that provides administrative and practice management services to physicians and physician groups.

Managerial Accounting: That branch of accounting that focuses on budgeting and pricing.

Managerial Finance: the fiscal discipline that applies the principles of economics to resource allocation decision making in an organization. It is often referred to simply as finance.

Mandated Benefits: Benefits a health care plan is required by law to provide. Usually used to refer to less common health care benefits, such as in vitro fertilization. Self-funded plans are exempt from these benefits under ERISA.

Manual Rates: Used to determine the premium for a small group, mortality rates that are based on the experience of an average group.

Manufacturer Brands: Brands created and identified with a particular manufacturer.

Manufacturers' Agents: Middlemen who sell similar products for several noncompeting producers for a commission on what is actually sold.

Margin: Revenues less expenses.

Marginal Analysis: Evaluation of the change in total revenue and total cost in selling one more unit in order to find the most profitable price and quantity.

Marginal Cost: The incremental cost per unit, consisting of the variable cost per unit plus any other changes in total direct cost associated with the additional unit of output.

Marginal Profit: The profit on the last unit sold.

Marginal Revenue: The change in total revenue that results from the sale of one more unit of a product.

Markdown: A retail price reduction that is required because customers won't buy an item at the original price.

Market: A group of potential customers with similar needs who are willing to exchange something of value with sellers offering various goods or services.

Marketable Securities: Investments that are readily marketable, hence are liquid. Examples include Treasury securities, large CDs, other money market instruments, and listed equity securities.

Market Aggregation: A marketing strategy that uses a single marketing program to offer the same product to all consumers.

Market Area: The geographic area in which enrollees reside.

Market Atomization: A marketing strategy that treats each consumer as a unique market segment.

Market Clearing Price: See *market equilibrium*.

Market Development: Attempt to increase sales by selling present products in new markets.

Market-Directed Economic System: Situation in which individual decisions of many producers and consumers make macro-level decisions for the whole economy.

Market Division: An arrangement whereby competitors divide territories or customers among themselves.

Market Equilibrium: The conditions under which supply and demand are in balance, generally characterized by a single price known as a market clearing price.

Market Growth: A stage of the product life cycle when industry sales grow fast, but when industry profits rise and then start falling.

Market Information Function: The collection, analysis, and distribution of all the information needed to plan, carry out, and control marketing activities.

Marketing Audit: A systematic, critical, and unbiased review and appraisal of the basic objectives and policies of the marketing function and of the organization, methods, procedures, and people employed to implement the policies.

Marketing Company Era: A time when, in addition to short-run marketing planning, marketing people develop long-range plans—sometimes 10 or more years ahead—and the whole company effort is guided by the marketing concept.

Marketing Concept: The idea that an organization should aim all its efforts at satisfying its customers, at a profit.

Marketing Department Era: A time when all marketing activities are brought under the control of one department to improve short-run policy planning and to try to integrate the firm's activities.

Marketing Ethics: The moral standards that guide marketing decisions and actions.

Marketing Information System (MIS): An organized way of continually gathering and analyzing data to provide marketing managers with information they need to make decisions.

Marketing Management Process: The process of planning marketing activities, directing implementation of the plans, and controlling these plans.

Marketing Mix: The combination of activities involving product, price, place, and promotion that a firm undertakes in order to provide satisfaction to consumers in a given market.

Marketing Model: A statement of relationships among marketing variables.

Marketing Orientation: The tendency of an organization to try to carry out the marketing concept.

Marketing Plan: A written statement of a marketing strategy and the time-related details for carrying out the strategy.

Marketing Program: A course that blends all of the firm's marketing plans into one big plan.

Marketing Research Process: A five-step application of the scientific method that includes defining the problem, analyzing the situation, getting problem-specific information, interpreting the data, and solving the problem.

Marketing Research: Procedures to develop and analyze new information to help marketing managers make decisions.

Marketing Strategy: Specification of a target market and a related marketing mix.

Market Introduction: A stage of the product life cycle when sales are low, as a new idea is first introduced to a market.

Market Maturity: A state of the product life cycle when sales are stable, as no incrementally new buyers seek to purchase the product.

Market Penetration: Attempt to increase sales of a firm's present products in its present markets, usually through a more aggressive marketing mix.

Market Potential: The quantity of a product or service that a whole market segment might buy.

Market Power: The ability to profitably maintain prices above competitive levels, or restrain output, for a significant period.

Market Rate: Any rate of return determined in a competitive market.

Market Segment: A relatively homogeneous group of customers who will respond to a marketing mix in a similar way.

Market Segmentation: A two-step process of naming broad product markets and segmenting them in order to select target markets and develop suitable marketing mixes.

Market Share: The percentage of total sales in the relevant market attributable to an individual business entity.

Market Skimming Strategy: Establishment of the highest price possible with the realization that certain segments of the market will pay it. When sales slow, the price is dropped to attract another level of purchaser.

Market Value: The amount of money that a good, service, or resource may be expected to attract if offered in the marketplace.

Markup: A dollar amount added to the cost of products to get the selling price.

Markup Chain: The sequence of markups firms use at different levels in a channel by which the price structure in the whole channel is determined.

Maser: Microwave amplification by stimulated emission of radiation.

Mass Marketing: The typical production-oriented approach that vaguely aims at everyone with the same marketing mix.

Mass-Merchandising Concept: The idea that retailers should offer low prices to get faster turnover and greater sales volume by appealing to larger markets.

Mass Selling: Communicating with large numbers of potential customers simultaneously.

Master Budget: The total budget package of an organization, including both operational and financial budgets.

Master Contract: A legally binding agreement between the insurer and the group policyholder to which insured individuals are not parties.

Matching Convention: In accounting, the practice of recognizing expenses in the same period in which recognition is given to the revenues associated with those expenses.

Matching Principle of Financing: The belief that short-term financial needs should be satisfied through short-term sources and that long-term needs should be satisfied through long-term sources.

Material Item: Any item of sufficient significance to the financial depiction of an organization that it must be included in financial statements under GAAP.

Material Misrepresentation: A misstatement that, had the truth been known, the insurer would either have not written the policy or would have written it with different terms and conditions.

Matrix Management: An organizational structure in which individuals may have two different reporting relationships (e.g., functional and professional).

Maturity: The date on which a financial obligation, such as the principal on a bond or note, becomes due.

Maturity Value: See *face value*.

Maximum Allowable Charge: The highest allowed charge from a vendor. Related to fee maximum. The term is often used in fee-for-service physician practice and in pharmacy contracting.

MBA: Master's degree in business administration.

MBHCO: Managed behavioral health care organization.

MCO: Managed care organization.

MDC: Major diagnostic categories.

Measure of Damages: The extent of loss or injury for which the law allows recovery.

Mediation: The nonbinding use of a third party in negotiations, usually after the parties to the negotiations have been unable to resolve differences on one or more elements of the negotiations.

Medicaid: A program that, if elected by a state or similar jurisdiction in accordance with federal legislation, pays for health care services for some poor and indigent persons. Specifics of Medicaid programs are established at both the federal and state levels, and funding is a joint federal-state undertaking under state management.

Medical Application: Inclusion in the insurance application of a section that must be completed by a physician after examination of the applicant.

Medical Audit: Any of several quality measurement techniques that use a systematic analysis of medical records data and lists of defined criteria for specific diagnoses and disease or injury states.

Medical Care Component: The category of the consumer price index (CPI) that tracks inflation in prices for health care in the United States.

Medical Care Value Purchasing: The use of mutually agreed-upon standards of cost and quality by buyers and sellers of health care services in the market for health care contracts.

Medical Computer Science: The branch of computer science that deals with medical applications.

Medical Effectiveness: See *effectiveness*.

Medical Examination: Physical examination of a potential insured conducted by a physician.

Medical Expense Coverage: A form of health insurance that provides benefits to help the insured pay for expenses incurred in the treatment of illness or injury.

Medical Illness Severity Grouping System (MedisGroups): A proprietary severity-of-illness indexing system trademarked by MediQual Systems, Inc., Westborough, Mass.

Medical Informatics: Study of the management and use of biomedical information.

Medical Information Science: See *medical informatics*.

Medical Information Systems: Any equipment or procedures used for the collection, recording, processing, storage, retrieval, and display of clinical information.

Medical Loss Ratio: The ratio between the cost to deliver medical care and the amount of revenue a plan receives. If rates are too low, the ratio may be high, even though the cost of delivering care is not excessive.

Medical Management: A specialty of medicine characterized by practitioner involvement in the operations and direction of health care and other enterprises.

Medical Quality Management: Systems and procedures for defining, measuring, monitoring, and improving the quality of care provided in a health care organization.

Medical Record: The format, sometimes electronic, in which all information on a patient and his or her encounters with a health care organization are recorded. Refers to the individual encounter and to the sum of an individual's encounters with the organization.

Medical Records Review: See *medical audit*.

Medical Service Organization (MSO): Entity that provides administrative support to clinical practices.

Medical Staff: Professional medical personnel who provide care to patients in a facility, institution, or agency.

Medical Staff Bylaws: A legal document that describes the organization, roles, and responsibilities of the medical staff.

Medical Staff Executive Committee: The chief policy-making body of the medical staff. Members are elected or selected by the medical staff and make recommendations to the organization's governing body on the basis of reports and recommendations from other medical staff committees.

Medicare: A federal program that pays for health care services for eligible elderly and disabled persons and persons with renal failure. It is funded by a combination of federal payroll taxes, general revenue, and premiums from enrollees in one part of the program and is administered by the Health Care Financing Administration of the Department of Health and Human Services.

Medicare Part A: The part of the federal program that pays for a portion of the cost of inpatient services at hospitals and certain posthospitalization services for Medicare beneficiaries.

Medicare Part B: The part of the federal program that pays for a portion of the cost of physician services rendered to inpatients and outpatients and of outpatient services rendered by hospitals and others for Medicare enrollees.

Medico-Economics: Economic aspects of the field of medicine, the medical profession, and health care. It includes the economic and financial impact of disease in general on the patient, the physician, society, or government.

Medigap: Health care insurance purchased from carriers to supplement Medicare beneficiaries' coverage

MedisGroups: See *Medical Illness Severity Grouping System.*

Medlars: Medical Literature Analysis and Retrieval System.

Medline: An on-line literature database on medical sciences and health care management topics maintained by the National Library of Medicine. Medlars on-line.

Member Months: The number of months each member of a prepaid health plan was covered. For example, if a plan had 10,000 members in January and 12,000 in February, the total member months as of March 1 would be 22,000.

Memory: Areas of the computer that are used for storage of data and software program.

Mentoring: The process by which an experienced professional helps less experienced colleagues gain experience and confidence in a profession.

Menu: A list of options from which the user may select programs or program elements.

Menu-Driven: Describes software program that is operated through selection from a series of menu options.

Merchant Wholesalers: Wholesalers who own (take title to) the products they sell.

MeSH: Medical subject headings, used by *Medlars* and *Medline*.

Message Channel: The carrier of a message.

Meta-Ethics: An analysis of the language, concepts, and objectives of ethics.

MGMA: Medical Group Management Association.

MHTS: Multiphasic health testing services.

MIA: Multi-institutional arrangement.

Micro-Allocation: A form of rationing. The determination of who should receive resources, as opposed to macro-allocation, another form of rationing, in which a determination is made on how much to spend on resources and what resources to make available.

Microcomputer: The smallest and least expensive computers, these devices use microprocessors as their central processing units.

Micro-Macro Dilemma: The principle that what is good for some producers and consumers may not be good for society as a whole.

Micro-Marketing: Activities that seek to accomplish an organization's objectives by anticipating customer or client needs and directing a flow of need-satisfying goods and services from producer to customer or client.

Microprocessor: The basic control devices for microcomputers and other small computer devices, these integrated circuit chips contain the arithmetic, logic, and control elements required for data processing.

Middleman: Someone who specializes in trade rather than production.

Minicomputer: The midrange of computers, fitting in size, cost, and complexity between microcomputers and mainframes.

Minimum Premium Plan: A group health insurance plan that is partially self-funded by the policyholder but administered by another firm, usually an insurance company.

Minimum Wage: The hourly amount that must be paid for labor as defined and established by federal law and regulations.

MIS: Management information system.

Mission: The basic purpose of an organization, that is, what it is trying to accomplish.

Misstatement of Age or Sex Provision: The right of the insurer to modify benefits if a misstatement by the insured on age or sex has resulted in an incorrect premium.

Mixed Model: A managed care plan with two or more delivery systems. Can be closed or open panel system.

MMM: Master's degree in medical management.

MMWR: Morbidity and Mortality Weekly Report.

Mode of Premium Payment: The frequency—annually, semiannually, quarterly, monthly, etc.—with which premiums are paid.

Modem (Modulator-Demodulator): A peripheral device that translates computer digital data into analog signals for telephone transmission to external computers and computer-driven devices.

Modified Cash Accounting: A variation on cash-basis accounting in which certain noncash items (e.g., depreciation) are included in the financial statements.

Modified Rebuy: The in-between process where some review of the buying situation is done, though not as much as in new-task buying or as little as in straight rebuys.

Modular System: A computer system composed of separate units, each of which performs a specific set of functions.

Money: Any physical or electronic medium established by a society, typically via its government, as the common denominator for all exchanges of real resources, financial assets, and goods and services. Money results from a social covenant among members of the society in which all agree to accept quantities of that money for all other items of value such as those noted above. Hence, money becomes a temporary store of value for those who hold it and, in a market economy, is the "ticket" that allows access to consumption.

Money Market Fund: A mutual fund holding a portfolio of money market instruments, such as Treasury bills and CDs.

Monitor: The video display unit of a computer workstation.

Monopolization: Willful acquisition or maintenance of monopoly power in a relevant market.

Monopoly: A market in which a single organization controls the supply of a good or service.

Monopoly Power: The ability of a single seller to fix or control prices, or to exclude competition (actual or potential), in a relevant market.

Monopsony: A market in which a single organization controls the demand for a good or service.

Moral Decision: A decision made after weighing its ethical consequences.

Moral Evaluation: Determination of an action to be taken based on moral standards set by society.

Moral Hazard: The risk of an insured's concealing pertinent information.

Moral Obligation: Standing behind a promise or taking an action on the basis of values set by society. See *moral responsibility*.

Moral Problems: Problems that present a clash of rights or values.

Moral Reference Group: People in a society who set standards that others follow.

Moral Reflection: An attempt to establish a social consensus on values when one does not exist. It requires social agreement about prioritization of competing human values and moral problem-solving.

Moral Responsibility: Belief that a moral principle is the basis for accountability. More flexible than moral obligation because it leaves room for discretion in a decision.

Moral Rights: Rights that are universal, equal, inalienable, and natural, as opposed to legal.

Morals: A general set of norms or mores from which people derive a sense of right and wrong. Social conscience.

Morbidity: Epidemiological term for the statistical incidence of disease states in a given population, usually expressed as the number of cases per 100,000 population. Generally, any disease state. Also refers to complications of any disease, test, or procedure.

Morbidity Rate: Incidence of sickness or injury in selected groups.

Morbidity Table: A chart of morbidity rates.

Mortality: Epidemiological term for the statistical incidence of death in a given population. Usually expressed in cases per 100,000 population for a specific disease or injury state. Also refers to death due to disease, test, or procedure.

Mortality Data: Information gathered by federal and state governments to permit comparisons of hospital performance.

Mortality Rate: The frequency with which death occurs in defined groups of people.

Mortgage Bond: A bond having real assets pledged as collateral.

Mortgage: A claim on a borrower's real assets given in exchange for a loan.

Mouse: A device that works with software programs to move data or other objects on the monitor screen, to select from menu options, and generally to operate the cursor.

MRI: Magnetic resonance imaging.

Multi-Option Plan: An employer health plan that allows employees to select from multiple coverage types, usually preferred provider organization, health maintenance organization, and indemnity plan.

Multiple Buying Influence: Situation in which the buyer shares the purchasing decision with several people, perhaps even top management.

Multiple Employer Welfare Association (MEWA): A group of employers who unite to purchase group health insurance, often through a self-funded plan, to avoid state mandates and insurance regulations.

Multiple Target Market Approach: Segmentation of the market and then treatment of individual segments as separate target markets needing a different marketing mix.

Multiple-Employer Groups: Groups consisting of the employees of two or more employers. See *Taft-Hartley groups*, *multiple-employer trusts*, and *voluntary trade associations*.

Multiple-Employer Trusts: The banding together of several small employers to provide group insurance for employees. In most cases, the employers belong to the same or to related industries. Also called multiple-employer welfare associations.

Multiple-Option Plan: A group plan that gives members a choice of product.

Multiprocessing: The simultaneous processing of two or more sets of instructions by multiple central processing units under common control.

Multiprogramming: Shared and simultaneous operation of two or more programs by a single computer.

Multi-Voting: A technique for narrowing a list of ideas to the most important entries.

Mutual Company: A health insurance company owned by policyholders and owners rather than stockholders.

N

National Association of Insurance Commissioners (NAIC): A voluntary organization of state insurance department commissioners whose purpose is promoting standardization and exchanging information among the states.

National Committee for Quality Assurance (NCQA): The primary accrediting body for managed care organizations. Its primary emphasis is on clinical quality and service quality improvement. See *HEDIS*.

National Health Board: Under managed competition, this board would collect information on outcomes, pricing, and quality for consumer use and would set risk adjustment factors. It also would design a standardized benefit plan according to federal guidelines.

National Health Insurance: Any of several proposals made over the years for ensuring that all citizens have access to health care services. Usually entails both financing and delivery mechanisms.

National Organ Transplant Act: Passed in 1984, this act established the 25-member multidisciplinary Task Force on Organ Procurement and Transplantation; makes funding available for not-for-profit regional organ procurement and transplantation organizations, including the National Donor Registry; and prohibits organ purchases in interstate commerce.

National Practitioner Data Bank (NPDB): Created by the Health Care Quality Improvement Act of 1986, the NPDB is a federal repository of information on disciplinary actions and malpractice claims histories for all U.S. physicians.

National Standard Rule: A test used for measuring the required level of care for a patient. It is based on the level of care provided by similar practitioners throughout the country. See *locality rule*.

Natural Death Acts: Statutes enacted in many states that establish procedures by which a competent individual can make provision for the withholding or withdrawing of medical therapy at the time when he or she loses the capacity to make such medical decisions. Natural death acts were enacted, in large part, to codify the increasingly popular living wills.

Needs: The basic forces that motivate a person to do something. Needs of health organizations are most often described in terms of what the professional thinks the patient (employee, donor, supplier, or any other constituent) requires to achieve or maintain basic existence.

Negative Exchange: Situation in which potential constituents have a negative attitude toward making the desired exchanges with an organization and deliberately avoid it.

Negligence: Failure to exercise that degree of care expected of a reasonably prudent person under similar circumstances. Active negligence occurs when one engages in conduct that causes injury. Passive negligence is the failure to act in fulfillment of a duty of care.

Negligence Per Se: Negligence that is recognized as such without proof as to the particular circumstances because it is so obviously contrary to accepted standards of prudence that no reasonable person would have engaged in it. Conduct that is a violation of a specific statute is also "negligence per se."

Negligence Theory: A theory of informed consent based on a physician's breach of duty to disclose relevant information as to a patient's illness and the risks, alternatives, and benefits of the procedure being recommended. Most states recognize this theory either by case law or statute. To involve negligence, a situation must meet the following criteria: a patient/physician relationship exists; the physician is bound to disclose relevant information; the physician inexcusably fails to provide the information; and the patient's injury or damage is a consequence of insufficient information.

Negotiated Contract Buying: Agreement to a contract that allows for changes in the purchase arrangements.

Negotiated Discount: Method of reimbursement for manage care providers that specifies percentage reductions in charges.

Negotiated Fee Schedule: Agreement by physicians to treat PPO patients at lesser charges than non-PPO patients. Also, the list of reduced fees for PPO services.

Negotiated Price: A price that is set on the basis of bargaining between the buyer and seller.

Negotiation: The process of bargaining in order to arrive at an agreement or compromise on a matter of importance to the parties involved.

Net: The final result after all reductions and adjustments have been made. For example, net revenue is obtained by subtracting allowances, deductions, and/or provisions from gross revenue. Net income is equal to net revenue plus other income minus all expenses and taxes. Net cash flow is the difference between cash inflows and cash outflows during a given period. An invoice term meaning that payment for the face value of the invoice is due immediately.

Net Lease: An arrangement in which the lessee assumes all ownership risks, including maintenance, upkeep, and taxes.

Net Loss Ratio: See *medical loss ratio*.

Net Premium: Rate based only interest and mortality rates. Also a rate that has been calculated without considering the insurer's business expenses.

Net Present Value: The difference between the present value of cash inflows and the present value of cash outflows specific to a particular proposal using a discount rate consistent with the risk characteristics of those cash flows; the economic value created by a decision; pure economic profit.

Net Profit: The earnings of a company from its operations during a particular period.

Net Sales: The actual sales dollars a company receives.

Network: Group of providers contractually linked to provide a full range of health care services. Open network allows beneficiaries access to other providers at greater cost. Closed network allows beneficiaries no access to other providers.

Net Working Capital: The difference between current assets and current liabilities.

Net Worth: The difference in value between an individual's assets and liabilities. For a corporation or other entity, its equity or fund balances.

Network Model HMO: Health plan that contracts with two or more physician groups for the provision of care to members.

Network Protocol: The rules or conventions that govern the preparation and transmission of data in a communication network.

Network Topology: The configuration of the physical connections in a computer communication network.

New Product: A product that is new in any way for the company concerned.

New-Task Buying: Point where an organization has a new need and the buyer wants a great deal of information.

New Unsought Products: Products offering really new ideas that potential customers don't know about yet.

NIH: National Institutes of Health.

No Balance Billing: When physicians agree under a plan to accept what the plan reimburses and not try to collect the remainder from patients.

Node: A terminal, station, communication computer, or other device in a network.

Noise: Any unwanted, spurious, or otherwise unintended signal in a device or system. Any distraction that reduces the effectiveness of the communication process.

Nominal Damages: An award that is of insignificant value. However, it reflects the fact that there has been an invasion of a party's rights even though no real damage resulted.

Nonadopters: Persons or organizations that prefer to do things the way they were done in the past. They are very suspicious of new ideas and do not purchase new products. See *adoption curve*.

Noncancellable Health Insurance Policy: A policy for which the premium cannot be changed and that must be renewed until the insured reaches a specified age if premiums are paid as due.

Noncontributory Plan: A group insurance plan for which insured members pay no portion of the costs.

Noncontrollable Services: Services rendered outside the service area.

Noncumulative Quantity Discounts: Reductions in price when a customer purchases a larger quantity on an individual basis.

Noncuperative Will: Oral statement, intended as a lawful will, made by someone near death.

Nonduplication of Benefits Provision: A limit on benefits payable when the insured is covered by two or more plans. The amount payable by the secondary plan is limited to any difference between the amount paid by the primary plan and the amount that would have been paid by the secondary plan had it been the primary plan. See *coordination of benefits (COB) provision*.

Noneconomic Damages: A term that is used to describe those elements of injury or loss that cannot easily and accurately be calculated in terms of money damages. For example, noneconomic losses might include pain and suffering, while economic losses would include lost wages.

Nonmaleficence: A principle that guides people and organizations to avoid harming others.

Nonmedical Application: A health insurance application form that does not require that the proposed insured be examined by a physician but instead contains health questions that the insured must answer.

Nonoperating Expenses: Expenses associated with transactions or activities incidental to an organization's main business.

Nonoperating Income: The difference between revenues and expenses for transactions or activities incidental to an organization's main business.

Nonoperating Revenues: Revenues associated with transactions or activities incidental to an organization's main business.

Nonparticipating Provider: Health care provider who has not contracted with a carrier or a health plan to provide services to members.

Nonprice Competition: Aggressive marketing action on the basis of product, place, or promotion rather than price.

Nonprofit: Designation for an organization that may engage in only certain economic activity (e.g., educational services, health care services) and is barred, by law, from distributing any of its assets or profits to private persons for other than the market value of their services to the organization. Sometimes called *not-for-profit*.

Nonrecurring: A revenue or expense that is not expected to be repeated on a regular basis.

Nonverbal Communication: Body positioning, gestures, gesticulation, and other means of communicating attitude and thinking that do not involve words.

Norm: Any measure or standard of performance, usually statistically validated.

Normalization: Adjustment of a floating point quantity so that the fraction is within a prescribed range.

Normative Ethics: Theories that formulate and defend basic moral principles and rules that determine what is right or wrong.

Nosocomial: Disease or injury that is introduced to the patient after hospitalization.

Not-for-Profit: See *nonprofit*.

O

Objective Component: Evaluation of the competency of health care professionals and of their attitudes to patients' ethical concerns, values, and issues. Also evaluation of hospital management related to administrative and medical operational systems to ensure effectiveness and efficiency.

Objectives: The expressed purposes, missions, and goals of an organization or its units as established through administrative processes.

Object-Oriented Program: A programming technique that uses computer code to produce reusable objects that act in a definable way rather than the traditional method of computer code that defines instructions for acting upon a data element.

Obligations: Binding duties stemming from ethical principles, professional commitments, or actions.

OBRA: Omnibus Budget Reconciliation Act. Laws passed by Congress as part of its budget reconciliation process. In 1987, for instance, OBRA dealt with requirements for care provided in nursing homes. See *COBRA*.

Office of Managed Care: Agency of the U.S. Department of Health and Human Services responsible for directing the federal HMO program. Previously known as the Office of Health Maintenance Organizations.

Office of Prepaid Health Care Operations and Oversight (OPH-COO): The federal agency, which is part of HCFA, that oversees qualification and compliance for HMOs and eligibility for CMPs.

OFI: In continuous quality improvement, an opportunity for improvement.

Old Age, Survivors, Disability and Health Insurance Act (OASDHI): Federal legislation that provides pension and long-term disability income to Americans. Also known as Social Security.

OLE (Object Linking and Embedding): The process by which an object from one computer application may be shared with another, eliminating the need to recreate the object. This technology allows changing of the new object to update the old.

Oligopoly: A special market situation that develops when a market has essentially homogeneous products, relatively few sellers, and fairly inelastic industry demand curves.

Oligopsony: A market for a specific good or service in which a few buying organizations are dominant as a group but not individually.

OMB: Office of Management and Budget.

On-line: Connected to and communicating directly with the computer's central processing unit.

Open Access: Ability of patients to see participating providers without approval of gatekeeper.

Open-Ended HMO: Plan in which enrollees can utilize services outside the HMO provider network without referral authorization, but must pay an extra copayment and/or deductible. Also called point-of-service plan

Open Enrollment Period: The stipulated time during which enrollees in a group contract must select a health plan alternative. Under federal HMO regulations, HMOs must allow at least 30 days.

Open Network: See *network*.

Open Panel: A managed care plan that contracts with private physicians who deliver care from their offices.

Operating Budget: Projections of expected revenues and expenses for an organization in the normal course of its activities.

Operating Expenses: Expenses incurred in the normal business of an organization.

Operating Income: Operating revenues minus operating expenses; also called operating margin.

Operating Lease: A cancelable lease covering a period shorter than the expected useful life of the leased asset. Maintenance of the asset is typically the responsibility of the lessee, and the lessee treats lease payments as expenses. Neither the leased asset nor recognition of its underlying financing appears on the balance sheet of the lessee. Sometimes called a "service lease." See *net lease*, and *contrast with capital lease*.

Operating Margin: See *operating income*.

Operating Ratio: Any of a number of financial ratios (e.g., asset turnover, average collection period) that provide some indication of an organization's operational characteristics.

Operating Revenues: Revenues recognized in the normal business of an organization.

Operating Statement: A simple summary of the financial results of a company's operations over a specified period.

Operating System: Software that controls the execution of computer programs and provides numerous housekeeping, accounting, and data management services.

Operational (Cash) Flows: All disbursements and receipts of an organization other than those between the organization and its capital suppliers (capital cash flows).

Operational Accountability: See *accountability*.

Operational Decisions: Short-run decisions to help implement strategies.

Opinion Leader: A person who influences others.

Opportunity Cost: The value forgone by selecting one course of action over the next best (or a baseline) course of action. The benefits that are not gained or the marginal costs that are accrued by the failure to take a specific course of action.

Optical Character Reader (OCR): An input device that reads characters on printed documents by their shapes, translating them into machine language for further manipulation.

Optical Disk: A high-density storage device that uses laser technology.

Option: The legal right to buy or to sell an asset at or within a given time at a given (exercise) price. See *call* and *put*.

Optional Insured Rider: See *second insured rider*.

Optionally Renewable Health Insurance Policy: Individual policy that is renewable on the anniversary date only at the insurer's discretion.

Opt-out Product: A health plan that gives enrollees the option of selecting another plan at a future time.

Ordinary Means of Treatment: Medical care that includes medicine, treatments, and procedures that offer heath improvement and that can be obtained and used without excessive pain.

Orthogenic Genetics: The study of how organisms change independently of external factors.

OSHA: Occupational Safety and Health Administration, Occupational Safety and Health Act of 1970.

Outcome Assessment: Evaluation procedures that focus on the status of the patient at the end of an episode of care.

Outcome Indicators: Specific definitions and measures of the anticipated results of given treatments or procedures that can be used to assess performance within or across health care organizations.

Outcome Rate: A statistical expression of the rate at which patients undergoing specific treatments or procedures achieve the desired outcomes.

Outcomes: The measured and recorded results of clinical diagnoses, treatments, and procedures. Outcomes also include morbidity, mortality, changes in functional status or health status, and satisfaction.

Outcomes Management: See *clinical outcomes management*.

Outcomes Research: Studies of the impact of health care interventions on results and costs.

Outflow: See *disbursement*.

Outlay: See *disbursement*.

Outliers: Providers or organizations whose outcomes overall or for specific disease or injury classifications are outside established norms.

Out-of-Area Benefits: The range of emergency benefits to which HMO members are entitled when outside their defined service areas. Emergency coverage is one of the few HMO benefits for which members might need to pay out of pocket and file claims to get reimbursed.

Out-of-Pocket Costs: The portion of health care costs paid directly by the patient.

Outpatient: Patient who receives health care services outside the hospital setting.

Output Device: Printers, plotters, and other units for display of computer data.

Ova Banking: Storing fertile eggs for future use in producing a human baby.

Overhead Costs: Any expense that cannot be directly attributed to the provision of a service or to the production of a good; in short, referred to as "overheads."

Overinsurance Provision: Individual policy provision that specifies under what conditions benefits are reduced when the insured has more insurance than is needed to cover medical expenses.

Overutilization: Provision of care in excess of established norms for specific disease or injury states.

P

Packaging: Promoting and protecting the product.

Pain and Suffering: An element of damages. In essence, it is the allowance of recovery for the physical pain one has had to endure and its subsequent mental sequelae. The term may also be used in some jurisdictions to describe mental trauma absent physical pain.

Paper Profit (Loss): See *unrealized gain (loss)*.

Parallel Processing: Simultaneous execution of two or more processes in multiple devices.

Paramedical Examination: A physical examination conducted by other than a physician.

Parens patriae: The power of the government to protect an individual for his or her own good.

Pareto Chart: A chart in which bars are used in ascending or descending order (from left to right or from top to bottom) to reflect the frequency or intensity of specific items. In quality management, the bars usually represent specific problems or processes within a system.

Pareto Principle: The observation that, in the relationship between cause and effect, the bulk of the effect is the result of a small number of causes. Also called the 80-20 rule, wherein 80 percent of the effect derives from 20 percent of the causes.

Par Provider: Abbreviated term for participating provider. Term for provider who has signed an agreement to provide services to plan members.

Par Value: See *face value*.

Partial Hospital: Provision by a hospital of mental health or substance abuse programs as alternatives or follow up to inpatient care.

Participating Provider: A provider who contracts with a third-party payer—Medicare, Medicaid, insurer, or the like—to provide services to all patients who (1) seek services from that provider and (2) are covered by that third party and accepts as payment in full for those services an amount agreed upon that is typically less than the usual charge of the provider. The provider may bill the patient only for whatever portion of the agreed-to amount is not paid by the third party. In Medicare, participating physicians are paid a premium relative to nonparticipating physicians. In HMOs, there may be restrictions, such as prior authorization of a referral.

Participative Budgeting: An approach to operating budgets in which those individuals and organizational elements affected by the budget are involved in its construction.

Partnership: A legal relationship between two or more competent parties that have contracted to place their money, effects, and labor in commerce or business with proportionate sharing of profits and losses.

Partnership Approach: When a managed care plan and provider work together to negotiate contracts.

Partnership: A contractual arrangement in which the parties to the contract agree to a method for sharing both expenses and revenues, for making capital contributions, and for receiving distributions of money. Partnerships are pass-through entities. One or more partners also bear personal liability for the debts of the partnership.

Passive Euthanasia: Withholding or refusing to provide treatment for a dying patient.

Pass-Through Entity: Organizations, such as S corporations and partnerships, the income (gains and losses) of which is attributed for income tax purposes directly to the organization's individual owners. The organization itself pays no income taxes, but the individual owners must pay taxes on attributed income even if those owners receive no cash distributions.

Paternalism: Furthering the well-being of others without necessarily having obtained their consent.

Patient: See *client and patient*.

Patient-Centered Care: Philosophical approach to care in which patients' perceived and expressed needs are the factors driving both the design and the operation of the care plans and systems.

Patient Dumping: Sending an ill or disabled person to a health care facility and forcing that facility to take responsibility for the person's welfare. Also known as patient diversion.

Patient Flow: Rate at which payers deliver patients to providers. Also rate at which providers complete individual patient sessions in ambulatory or emergency care.

Patient Management Categories (PMCs): A proprietary severity-of-illness indexing system trademarked by the Center for Health Services Research of the Pittsburgh Research Institute, Pittsburgh, Penn.

Patient Profile: Computer-based summary of key medical and demographic information on a given patient.

Patient Risk Adjusted Groupings, PRAGmatic System (PRAGs): A proprietary severity-of-illness indexing system trademarked by Corporate Cost Management, Gaithersburg, MD.

Patient Satisfaction: A measure of health, usually obtained through formal surveys of patients.

Patient's Bill of Rights: Adopted in 1973 and revised in 1992 by the American Hospital Association. It states, "The patient has the right to obtain from the physician current information concerning diagnosis, treatment, and prognosis in terms that the patient can be reasonably expected to understand."

Patient Transfer: Moving a patient from one health care facility or unit to another. Conditions of patient transfer are governed by several federal laws, including sections of Consolidated Omnibus Budget Reconciliation Acts and Omnibus Budget Reconciliation Act.

Patient Volume: The number of patients generated by plans for their preferred providers.

Patterns: See *practice patterns*.

Payable: An amount owed by an organization or individual to another for resources supplied to the former by the latter.

Payback Period: The time required for the total cash inflows from a project to equal the initial investment for the project. Calculated as initial investment divided by average annual cash inflow.

Payer: Person or entity providing funds for health care services.

Payment Audit Report: Information on the amount of expected reimbursement versus the amount of actual reimbursement by case, by contract.

Payment System: See *reimbursement system*.

Payroll Deduction: A payment mechanism under which the employer deducts premiums from the employee's paycheck and sends them to the insurance company.

PCP: See *primary care provider*.

PE: Physician executive.

Peer Grouping: An analytic technique that classifies physicians by specialty.

Peer Review: The formal process, including standards setting, measurement and monitoring, and evaluation, by which the quality of care provided by individual clinicians is measured and evaluated.

Peer Review Committee: A legally constituted group within an health care organization that evaluates and makes judgments on the quality of care provided by individual practitioners.

Peer Review Groups: Local physician groups that help solve claim disputes and promote fair and ethical practices in the health care industry.

Peer Review Improvement Act: The 1982 federal law that established peer review organizations.

Peer Review Organization (PRO): Replaced the Professional Standards Review Organization (PSRO) in 1982. Established by the federal Department of Health and Human Services (HHS) to review information submitted to state or federal fraud and abuse agencies; to federal and state agencies that identify public risks; and to state licensure or certification agencies. Not considered a federal agency. Licensed by the Health Care Financing Administration to oversee cost-effectiveness of care provided under the Medicare and Medicaid programs.

Penalty Provision: Reduction in benefits for failure to comply with plan requirements.

Penetration: Percentage of business an HMO captures in a market area.

Penetration Pricing Policy: Attempt to sell the whole market at one low price.

Per Capita: Per head; per person; the allocation of data in a statistic to all of the individuals who are affected by or who contribute to the statistic.

Per Case Payment: Payment to providers for the entire diagnostic episode rather than by individual service.

Per Cause Deductible: An amount that applies to all eligible expenses from a single illness or injury.

Per Diem Reimbursement: Payment to hospital based on a set rate per day rather than charges.

Per Diem: Per day; used to refer to any amount (e.g., total cost) for a given period divided by the number of days in that period; also a rate of payment in which total payment is proportionate to the number of days over which care was provided.

Per Member Per Month (PMPM): In managed care statistics, the allocation of various statistics to the individual member level on a monthly basis.

Per Se Violation: A term of antitrust law regarding violations, such as price fixing, that are so plainly anticompetitive that no elaborate study of the industry is necessary to establish their illegality and no justification is permitted on the basis of special circumstances in the particular market.

PERT: Program evaluation and review technique.

Per Thousand Members Per Year: A common way of reporting hospital utilization.

Percentage Participation: See *coinsurance.*

Perfect Market: Situation in which the quality and quantity of exchanges between an organization and one of its constituencies are exactly what is needed and desired. This is an inherently unstable situation, as both the exchanges themselves and the organization's idea of perfection are constantly changing.

Performance Agreement: An administrative contract in which minimum levels of payment and coding accuracy are detailed.

Performance Analysis: Analysis that looks for exceptions or variations from planned performance.

Performance Appraisal: Standards a plan sets for physicians that are broken down into categories such as productivity, medical charting, dependability, medical knowledge, management of patient care, attitude and leadership, and participation.

Performance Index: A number that shows the relation of one value to another.

Performance Measures: Quantitative measures of the specific elements of a process to determine their quality.

Performance Monitoring: See *clinical performance monitoring.*

Performance Reporting: The comparison of actual results with budgeted results.

Performance Scoring System: Methodology used to profile physicians.

Periodic Interim Payment: Lump sum payments to a provider by a third-party payer on the basis of expected use of services by subscribers or insureds. End-of-year adjustments are made to bring accounts into balance.

Peripheral Device: Printers, modems, FAX equipment, plotters, hard drives, and other devices connected to the central processing unit for the translation and/or transmission of data into more usable form.

Permanent Injunction: A court order to do or refrain from doing some act that is issued as part of the final judgment by the court in a lawsuit.

Persistent Vegetative State: A coma from which a person never wakes.

Personal Computer: A moderately priced microcomputer intended for personal rather than business use. See *microcomputer.*

Personal Contact: Communication device that can be achieved by having an organization's staff or supporters speak to public gatherings or by inviting members of other community organizations to visit the organization, or both.

Personal History Interview: A report that contains the same types of information as the inspection report except that the insured is the only source of information and the interview is conducted by insurer's employees rather than outside agencies.

Personal Needs: An individual's need for personal satisfaction that is unrelated to what others think or do.

Personal Selling: Direct spoken communication between sellers and potential customers, usually in person but sometimes over the telephone.

Personal Service Corporation: A corporation whose income is derived almost entirely from the personal services of shareholders; typically used for single-shareholder professionals such as physicians and dentists.

PGP: Prepaid group practice.

Pharmacoeconomics: Assessment of cost-effectiveness of drug therapy.

Pharmacy and Therapeutics Review: See *drug utilization review*.

Philosophy of Care: The mission statement of a health plan.

Philosophy: Theories and analysis of conduct, thought, and knowledge.

Physical Distribution (PD): The transporting and storing of goods so as to match target customers' needs with a firm's marketing mix, both within individual firms and along a channel of distribution.

Physical Distribution (PD) Concept: The principle that all transporting and storing activities of a business and a channel system should be coordinated as one system that should seek to minimize the cost of distribution for a given customer service level.

Physical Examination Provision: The right of the insurer to have the insured with a claim examined by a physician of the insurer's choice and at the insurer's expense.

Physician Contingency Reserve: See *withhold*.

Physician Credentialing: See *credentialing*.

Physician Hospital Organization (PHO): A legal entity formed by a hospital and a group of physicians to further mutual interests and to achieve market objectives. The PHO is typically owned and governed jointly by the hospital and physicians and serves as a collective negotiating and contracting unit.

Physician Incentive Plan: Compensatory plan designed to motivate physicians to restrain specialist referrals and use health care resources more efficiently. Also intended to aid in the physician recruitment process.

Physician Organization: A legal entity formed by physicians and/or physician groups for the purpose of negotiating contracts for the provision of services to groups of patients.

Physician Payment System: One of a variety of systems used by health plans to control costs and reward physicians who hold down costs. Examples include discounted fees, capped fee schedules, capped fee schedules with withhold, primary care capitation, and full capitation.

Physician Profiles: Presentation or display of data on the practice patterns of individual practitioners, emphasizing the economic impacts of those practices on the health care organization.

Physician Supply: At any given time, the number of physicians in a given market. The statistic is often refined to distinguish among licensure, active or retired, patient care or other activity, level of training or certification, specialty, age, sex, etc.

Piggyback System: A way of describing the managed care information system (MCIS). It does not support operational transactions, such as the hospital's order entry system. Rather, it extracts data from other systems and rapidly reformats them for reporting and analysis. Also referred to as a niche system.

Pioneering Advertising: Advertising that tries to develop primary demand for a product category rather than demand for a specific brand.

Pixel: The smallest unit on the monitor screen that can be stored, displayed, or addressed. The building block for computer graphics.

Place: Making goods and services available in the right quantities and locations and when customers want them.

Place Utility: The value to the customer of having the product available where the customer wants it.

Plaintiff: The one who initially brings a lawsuit.

Plan Design: The features included in a health plan.

Plan of Care: A strategy for implementing continuous quality improvement within the context of systems thinking. It is a designed path from entry into the health care system to an outcome. It represents a design-and-build effort to create a seamless system of care across many settings.

Plan-Do-Check-Act Cycle: A process for quality improvement developed for quality control by Walter Shewhart and adapted for total quality management by W. Edwards Deming.

Planning: The process of developing budgets and other plans for an organization.

Pleadings: The formal written documents, in legal format, filed with the court by the parties that set out the plaintiff's allegations (cause of action) and the defendant's answer to those allegations. Pleadings generally include the complaint, answer, response to affirmative defenses raised in the answer, third-party claims, cross claims, counterclaims, and the answer to each.

Pledging of Receivables: The use of anticipated payments on accounts receivable as collateral to obtain a loan.

Plow Back: The reinvesting in the organization's business of cash produced by that organization rather than returning that cash to capital suppliers.

Pluralism: Identifying more than one intrinsic good; the theory that reality is composed of more than one or two entities. Also, a doctrine or concept that advocates that people of diverse ethnic, racial, religious, or social groups retain their culture or beliefs while living elsewhere.

PMCs: See *patient management categories*.

Point of Service (POS): Plan by which members are able to choose how to receive services at time of need.

Point-of-Care System: A hospital information system that includes bedside terminals for the acquisition and storage of patient data.

Point-of-Service (POS) Model HMO: Also known as an open-ended HMO. It offers a transition product that includes features of HMOs and PPOs. Enrollees have the option of going outside the network and paying extra through copayments and deductibles.

Policy Dividend: See *dividend*.

Policy Reserve: A liability account that identifies the assets and future premiums that will be required for a policy to satisfy all claims on the policy.

Policy Summary: A document that contains legally required data regarding the specific policy being considered by an applicant.

Policyholder: The owner of a group policy.

Policyowner: The person or party who owns an individual insurance policy.

POMR: Problem-oriented medical record.

Population-Based Analysis: A study based on the health of enrollees residing in a specific service area.

Population-Based Care: The building of a health care system or enterprise and the provision of care on the basis of populations of patients rather than on individual patients.

Positioning: An approach that shows how customers locate proposed and/or present brands in a market.

Possession Utility: The value to the customer of obtaining a product and having the right to use or consume it.

Post: The process of recording transactions in accounting.

Posted Charges: The list price for health care and medical care goods and services.

Power: The capacity or ability to exercise control and authority.

Power of Attorney: A proxy directive that allows an individual to appoint another to make a decision on his or her behalf. See *durable power of attorney*.

PPI: See *producer price index*.

PPO: See *preferred provider organization*.

PPS: See *prospective payment system*.

Practice Guidelines: A scientifically determined set of specifications for the provision of care to typical patients in given disease or injury categories. Also commonly called practice parameters, or practice protocols.

Practice Patterns: For individual practitioners or groups of practitioners, the statistically determined tendency to diagnose, prescribe, treat, or perform procedures in a given fashion. Usually determined on the basis of geography.

Practice Profiling: Collection of data on physician performance and comparing them to established averages.

PRAGs: See *Patient Risk Adjusted Groupings, PRAGmatic System*.

Preadmission Certification: Requirement that members obtain authorization from the plan for inpatient or outpatient services at health facilities. Members who do not obtain this certification are penalized by the plan, which reimburses facilities at a lower rate and forces members to pay the difference.

Preadmission Review: Part of utilization management in which the managed care company ascertains if the treatment will improve the patient's condition, if it can be performed in a cost-effective manner, and if it is medically necessary. See *precertification*.

Preadmission Screening: Testing done prior to admission to a health facility.

Preauthorization: Permission from the plan for a patient to be admitted to a specific health care facility for which the plan would make the maximum reimbursement. Without this approval, the provider or subscriber could be subject to a penalty.

Precertification: Provision that requires the insured or his or her provider to check coverage for a specific treatment or procedure in advance. See *preauthorization.*

Precision: The degree of accuracy with which an observation matches the underlying condition. The exactness with which an operation is performed.

Predatory Practices: Intentionally setting premium rates substantially below the cost of delivering care. This tactic is usually employed when a plan starts up to quickly gain market share.

Predatory Pricing: The offering of a good or service at a price less than variable or incremental cost with the intent of damaging competitors by taking market share from them and/or causing them to experience unsustainable losses.

Preexisting Condition: Any illness or injury that existed prior to a member's joining a health plan. Until passage of the Health Insurance Portability and Accountability Act of 1996 (Kennedy-Kassenbaum Bill), payment for treatment of such illnesses or injuries was commonly disallowed.

Preexisting Conditions Provision: The specification that, until a policy has been in force for a certain period, no benefits will be paid for conditions present before issuance of the policy. Provisions were rendered impotent by passage of the Health Insurance Portability and Accountability Act of 1996 (Kennedy-Kassenbaum Bill).

Preferred Provider Arrangement (PPA): Similar to PPO, except employers rather than providers make the arrangements.

Preferred Provider Contracting: Contracting with physicians who agree to accept whatever the plan pays for treating its members.

Preferred Provider Organization (PPO): An arrangement in which selected care organizations (preferred providers) agree to provide care to selected populations (e.g., employer groups) at a discount from posted charges in exchange for receiving an expected volume of patients and/or prompt payment for services provided. Typically, the providers remain in a fee-for-service arrangement and so are not at risk for increases in volume. Covered persons are typically "channeled" to the preferred providers with economic incentives, such as lower copayments.

Preferred Risk: A person classified as above average risk, with the probability of a lower mortality rate, because of physical condition, health history, occupation, and/or life-style.

Preliminary Injunction: A court order to do, or to refrain from doing, some act that is issued during the course of a lawsuit and remains effective until the dispute is settled or judgment is reached.

Premium: One of a series of payments required by the insurer to put a policy into effect and continue it. The amount paid by or on behalf of a member for coverage under a health plan.

Prepaid Expense: In accounting, the recognition of a payment made for a resource one year or less in advance of the expected use of that resource.

Prepaid Group Practice: Capitated system for predetermined patient grouping by medical practice group.

Prepaid Health Plan: Plan that collects a premium and contracts to provide defined benefits package for that premium.

Prepaid Practice: A financial arrangement in which a physician or physician group is paid a lump sum for the provision of services to a subscriber group for a given period, regardless of the actual nature, quantity, or cost of those services.

Prepayment: See *prepaid expense*; also used to refer to payments for care under capitated (HMO) plans; any payment made or received before contractually due.

Prepayment Penalty: The amount of money that must be paid in addition to the amount of remaining principal if a loan is paid off before maturity.

Prepayment Review: Determination of appropriateness of treatment or procedure by third-party payer.

Preponderance of the Evidence: A test used by the fact finder (judge or jury) to determine which side has prevailed on a point under contention. Alternatively described as the greater weight of the evidence, it generally requires that one side prove that the fact at issue is more likely than not. It is in contrast to "clear and convincing evidence" and "proof beyond a reasonable doubt," which are progressively higher standards of proof.

Present Value: The value now of expected future cash flows, using an appropriate discount rate.

Present Value Factor: The factor that, when multiplied by a specified amount of money expected at a later date, generates a product that is the present value of that future amount of money.

President's Commission for the Study of Ethical Problems in Medicine and Biomedical and Behavioral Research: Created in 1982 by the President to investigate claims that physicians could harm or upset patients by explaining their conditions to obtain informed consent. The Commission's objective was to determine if adverse reaction occurs when information is revealed and to establish standards for the release of information to patients. Its findings contribute to sound health care decisions and help reveal the ethical and legal implications of informed consent between patient and physician.

Prestige Pricing: The practice of setting a rather high price to suggest high quality or high status.

Presumption: A legal concept by which an assumption is made that a fact exists based on the existence of another or other facts.

Preventive Care: Medical services offered by a plan to keep its population as healthy as possible and to diagnose and treat medical problems before they become serious.

Price: The revenue that is posted or listed for each unit of a good or service produced by an organization. What is charged for a product or service. The term "charge" is a synonym.

Price Control: Imposition of a legal maximum or minimum price, or both, such as allowables in Medicare or payment for services in Medicaid.

Price Discrimination: The practice of attempting to injure competitors by selling the same products to different buyers at different prices. Two conditions must be met for discrimination to occur: exactly the same products have different prices and production costs must be equal. Also, in order for firms to be guilty of price discrimination, markets must separable (e.g., senior discounts or pharmaceutical products).

Price-Earnings Ratio: The ratio given by an organization's price per share of common stock divided by the actual or estimated earnings per share in any given one-year period.

Price Fixing: An agreement, the purpose or effect of which is to raise, fix, depress, peg, or stabilize prices. This is a term used in federal antitrust statutes and applied to commodities in interstate commerce. Such cooperative setting of price levels or ranges by competitors is unlawful per se under the antitrust laws.

Price Leader: A seller who sets a price that all others in the industry follow.

Price Lining: The practice of setting a few price levels for a product line and then marking all items within these price levels.

Prima Facie: A principle to be followed unless there are other, overriding considerations.

Prima Facie Case: A case that appears to have enough evidence to prevail in a lawsuit if it is not contradicted by evidence proving otherwise.

Primary Care Network: Group of primary care physicians who join to provide care to patients who are members of given health plan.

Primary Care Physician: Physician who provides basic health services and manages access to specialists.

Primary Care Provider (PCP): Generally includes internists, pediatricians, family physicians, and general practitioners.

Primary Data: Information specifically collected to solve a current problem. Raw or original data collected during the delivery of care.

Prime Rate: The loan rate charged by commercial banks to their least risky ("best") customers.

Principal: The corpus of a loan; the amount borrowed; the amount of a loan still outstanding and unpaid; the portion of a loan payment that will reduce the amount of the loan still unpaid and outstanding.

Printer: An output device that produces hard copies of computer data.

Prior Authorization: See *precertification, preauthorization*.

Privacy Act. The Privacy Act of 1974 prohibits the federal government from disclosing an individual's records unless requested by the individual. Federal hospitals are bound by the Privacy Act's provisions regarding patient records.

Private Branch Exchange (PBX): A telephone switching center.

Private Brands: Brands created by middlemen; sometimes referred to as dealer brands.

Private Placement: See *direct placement*.

Private Review Agent: A utilization management company.

Privilege Denials: Refusal by the appropriate medical staff agency, at the conclusion of privileging process, to allow a clinician to practice in a health care organization.

Privilege Restrictions: Actions taken by the appropriate medical staff agency, at the conclusion of the privileging process or following a peer review, to limit the extent to which a practitioner may practice in an organization. Usually is used to deny an unqualified practitioner the ability to perform specified procedures or use certain treatment regimens.

Privileging: The entire process by which the qualifications of individual practitioners to practice are determined, evaluated, and judged and the right to practice in an organization is granted. In health care organizations, this is a function adjunct to the credentialing process.

PRO: *Professional review organization*.

Pro Forma Financial Statements: Forecast of any or all of the set of financial statements based on the assumption that budgeted targets for an organization or for some division or project within an organization will be realized during specified future periods.

Proactive Outreach: Concerted provider effort to reach patient populations or to provide specific health care services.

Probability: The likelihood of an event's occurring, usually expressed in mathematical terms.

Probationary Period: The period during which a new employee must wait for access to group insurance plans.

Procedural Due Process: Those rights that assure a fair and thorough consideration of an issue. These rights are generally provided for by the U.S. and state constitutions. See *due process*.

Process: The series of steps and tasks that are required to deliver a given product or service.

Process Measures: Variables associated with the internal steps of a process.

Producer Price Index (PPI): An index reported monthly by the Bureau of Labor Statistics of the U.S. Department of Labor. The index tracks the prices of selected resources used as inputs to production in the overall U.S. economy.

Product: The need-satisfying offering of a firm.

Product Advertising: Advertising that tries to sell a specific product.

Product Assortment: The set of all product lines and individual products that a firm sells.

Product Development: The process of offering new or improved products for present markets.

Product Emphasis: Marketing by letting the product speak for itself.

Production: The process by which an organization converts input resources (materials, labor, energy) into goods and services for sale and delivery to consumers.

Production Era: A time when a company focuses on production of a few specific products, perhaps because few of these products are available in the market.

Production Orientation: Practice of making whatever products are easy to produce and then trying to sell them.

Product Liability: The legal obligation of sellers to pay damages to individuals who are injured by defective or unsafe products.

Product Life Cycle: The stages a new product idea goes through from introduction to withdrawal.

Product Line: A set of individual products that are closely related.

Product Managers: Persons within an organization who manage specific products, often taking over jobs formerly handled by an advertising manager; sometimes called brand managers.

Product Market: A market of buyers with similar needs and sellers offering various close substitute ways of satisfying those needs.

Professional Autonomy: Freedom to make decisions. Physicians in private practice have the greatest autonomy, but, if they join a physician/hospital organization or go to work for or contract with a managed care company, that autonomy may be diminished.

Professional Disclosure Standard: The standard holds that adequate disclosure is determined by customary rules or traditional practices of the professional community of physicians, who are presumed to be in a privileged position to determine their patients' best interests. The standard establishes the topics to be discussed and the amount of information that should be disclosed on each topic in the physician-patient relationship.

Professional Ethics: Ethical principles set down by a group to govern professional practices for its members.

Professional Knowledge: Subjects, disciplines, and values leading to traditional improvement in health care.

Professional Liability: The legal responsibility that a practitioner has for the provision of care at acceptable levels of quality and performance.

Professional Review Organization (PRO): An organization that reviews the activities and records of health care providers, institutions, or groups in terms of appropriateness of utilization.

Professional Standards Review Organization (PSRO): Now defunct, these agencies performed the utilization review functions currently performed by peer review organizations.

Profiling: See *physician profiles*.

Profit: The excess of revenues over expenses in a single transaction. The aggregate of all such excesses (net of any shortfalls) in a given period is the profit or net income for that period.

Profitability Ratio: Any of a number of financial ratios (e.g., return on assets, return on equity) that provide some indication of the extent to which of an organization has a profit (is profitable).

Profit and Loss Statement: See *income statement*.

Profit Maximization Objective: An attempt to get as much profit as possible.

Profit Plan: See *master budget*.

Program Language: A formal language by which computer programs are specified for the computer hardware.

Program: A series of instructions that cause the computer to process data in a prescribed manner.

Progressive Rates: New rates implemented by some HMOs on a monthly, quarterly or semiannual basis. New or established enrollees are automatically subject to the new rates on their anniversary dates.

Promotion: Communication of information between seller and potential buyer or others in the channel to influence attitudes and behavior. In health care, promotion basically consists of communicating to potential patients the existence, availability, attributes, access, and price of services offered.

Prompt: A message from the computer that it is ready to accept the prescribed data or command.

ProPac: Prospective Payment Assessment Commission.

Proration: The allocation of a total amount using a percentage formula.

Prospective Payment System (PPS): A system that pays prospectively rather than by charges. The system under which Medicare determines payment for inpatient hospitalization on a prospective basis using DRGs.

Prospective Payment: Determination, in advance of actual provision of services, of the amount to be paid for those services, particularly in a regulatory setting such as the DRG system employed by Medicare. The provider bears the risk of increases in its costs of providing the services.

Prospectus: A formal legal document that describes in detail any major transaction proposed by an organization (such as the sale of securities, a merger, or the acquisition or spin-off of a business), along with full disclosures of all relevant aspects of the transactions, including forecasts of consequences of the transaction, risk factor, and legal implications.

Protherapeutic Authoritarianism: Advocacy or imposition of medical interventions by persons whose personality, motives, and methods are authoritarian.

Protocol: A listing of each step in a treatment or procedure in terms of the alternatives that exist for the clinical decision-making process.

Provider: Individual or organizational supplier of health care services.

Provider Income: Payment physicians receive from the plan.

Provider Network: A group of physicians and hospitals participating in a managed health care plan.

Provider Risk Sharing: Acceptance of provider of financial responsibility for provision of services.

Provider-Sponsored Network: Physician-directed and -controlled organizations that contract for patients directly with managed care organizations, businesses, and insurers. See *physician organization*.

Provision for Bad Debts: See *allowance* and *allowance for bad debts*.

Proximate Cause: An act or omission that naturally and directly produces a consequence. In some jurisdictions, for an act to be considered the proximate cause of a loss or injury, it must be proved that, but for the act or omission, the injury or loss would not have occurred.

Proxy: Written and legal authorization for one person to act on behalf or in place of another, such as in voting shares of common stocks.

Prudent Buyer: An individual or entity that operates as a purchaser in the marketplace, always attempting to achieve efficient trade-offs between maximizing value and minimizing costs. A concept used by companies paying for health care services for employees to ensure that medical care value is attached to purchasing decisions.

Prudent Man Rule: A legal requirement that any person functioning in a fiduciary role exercise the discretion and judgment expected of a prudent person.

PSRO: Professional standards review organization.

Psychographics: See *life-style analysis*.

Public Charity: Any organization with a broad base of public financial support and operating for charitable purposes.

Public Health Service Act: Legislation that requires HMOs to have quality assurance programs in order to be granted Medicare contracts.

Public Offering: The process and documentation surrounding the sale of securities to the public.

Public Relations: Communication with customers and noncustomers, including labor, public interest groups, stockholders, and the government in order to establish a positive relationship or to influence one or more of the publics to accept the communicating organization's point of view.

Publicity: Any unpaid form of nonpersonal presentation of ideas, goods, or services. In contrast to paid advertising, which is often unethical or illegal for certain health services, publicity may be acceptable because it is free and likely to promote use of specific health services without identifying a single provider organization, even if only one exists. Publicity may be geared to raising the public image of, awareness of, or respect for health organizations in general.

Pulling: Practice of using promotion to get consumers to ask middlemen for the product.

Punitive Damages: A sum of money awarded not to compensate the injured party, but to punish the tortfeasor and deter him or her and others from similar acts. It generally requires that the act be of a willful, wanton, or reckless nature. Contracts or statutes should specifically authorize such punitive monetary penalties.

Purchase-Oriented Care Report: A report compiled from utilization review, case management, quality assurance, and claims adjudication information for consumers and payers so they can make informed decisions.

Pure Competition: A market situation that develops when a market has homogeneous products, many buyers and sellers who have full knowledge of the market, and ease of entry for buyers and sellers.

Push Money (or prize money) Allowances: Allowances (sometimes called PMs or spiffs) given to retailers by manufacturers or wholesalers to pass on to the retailers' salesclerks for aggressively selling certain items.

Pushing: Using normal promotion effort—personal selling, advertising, and sales promotion—to help sell the whole marketing mix to possible channel members.

Put: An option to sell; the owner of the put has the right (but no obligation) to sell an asset or security at a specified price on (or before) a specified date; the writer of the put has the reciprocal obligation if the put is activated (exercised). The put provision (if any) of a bond gives the lender (bondholder) the right to surrender the bond for a specified dollar payment prior to its nominal maturity.

Q

QA: See *quality assurance*.

QALE: Quality-adjusted life expectancy.

QALY: Quality-adjusted life years

QAP: Quality assurance program.

QBE (Query by Example): A method of selecting various elements from a database, defining limits for these elements, and using them to sort through the database to create a report.

Q-Stage: A proprietary severity-of-illness indexing system trademarked by SysteMetrics/McGraw-Hill, Inc., Santa Barbara, Calif.

Qualified Deferred Compensation Plan: A plan that meets Internal Revenue Service requirements so that contributions are deductible for the employer and carry no current tax obligation for the employee.

Qualified Health Plans: Medicare HMOs with broader provider distribution that are specifically authorized to provide services under federal regulations.

Qualitative Research: Process of seeking in-depth, open-ended responses that cannot be quantified.

Quality: A measure of the degree to which a product or service meets established standards or satisfies the needs of customers. In health care, high quality involves optimal care, including both reasonable access and timeliness, from the appropriate provider in the most appropriate setting in the most appropriate manner for the patient's unique circumstances.

Quality-Adjusted Life Expectancy: Multiplication of the statistically determined life expectancy of a person by a percentage factor that takes into consideration the expected quality of that life, ranging from 100 percent (full health) to zero percent (death).

Quality-Adjusted Life-Year: The number of years of life at full health that would equal a given number of years at less than full health.

Quality Assessment: A formal mechanism for determining the degree to which a product or service conforms with established standards.

Quality Assurance (QA): A formal hospital program for the evaluation of medical quality. It is characterized by the establishment of standards against which the performance of practitioners is judged.

Quality Control: Largely an industrial quality management concept, the term refers to the statistical analysis of defects in products and services and its use to adjust processes to correct the defects.

Quality Council: In the continuous quality improvement approach, a committee of managers and other participants to oversee the entire quality management process.

Quality Enhancement: See *continuous quality improvement*.

Quality Improvement: See *continuous quality improvement*.

Quality of Life: A global assessment, largely personal, of an individual's ability to function at satisfactory levels and to achieve desired goals and objectives. See *health status*.

Quality Management: See *medical quality management*.

Quality Trilogy: A concept developed by quality pioneer J.M. Juran to describe three elements of quality management: planning (developing processes for products or services to meet customers' needs, quality control (ensuring adherence to product and process standards), and quality improvement (achievement of ever higher levels of performance).

Quantitative Research: Process of seeking structured responses that can be summarized in numbers, such as percentages, averages, or other statistics.

Quantity Discount: A reduction in the price for a good or service that is tied to the quantity or volume of the good or service purchased.

Query: A request for specific information from the computer.

Queue: An ordered list of jobs waiting for computer or peripheral unit execution.

Quick Assets: Assets that may be easily converted into cash.

Quick Ratio: See *acid test ratio*.

R

RACMA: Royal Australian College of Medical Administrators.

Random-Access Memory (RAM): The working memory of the computer, into which programs are loaded and then executed.

Random Sampling: Technique in which each member of the research population has the same chance of being included in the sample.

Raster Scan: A pattern of rows of dots on a monitor that form an image.

Rate Guarantee: Plan agreement with employer to retain the same premium rate for a specified period.

Rate Setting: Assigning specific prices for treatments and procedures for specific conditions and illnesses.

Rated Policy: A policy issued for a person considered more likely to have a loss. Normally, such a policy carries higher premiums, is issued with special limitations or exclusions, or both.

Rating: See *bond rating, community rating, credit rating, experience rating*.

Rating Agency: An independent organization that assesses the risk of organizations and/or their securities and assigns ratings reflecting those assessments, particularly in conjunction with debt contracts and the likelihood of the provisions of those contracts being fulfilled by the organizations.

Rationing: In economic theory, the process of allocating insufficient resources to excessive numbers of users. In health care, this translates into using economic principles to limit access to health care services.

Raw Materials: Unprocessed expense items that are moved to the next production process with little handling.

RBRVS: See *relative value scale*.

RCC: Literally, the ratio of charges to charges (or costs to charges). The ratio of initial patient charges for a specific program to total patient charges; the ratio of total patient costs to total patient charges.

RCCAC: Literally, the "ratio of Charges to Charges (or Costs to Charges) Applied to Costs (Charges): A reimbursement determination formula for a retrospective payment system that consists of multiplication of RCC by allowable costs or by patient charges. Either formulation produces the same result.

Read Only Memory (ROM): The portion of the computer's memory that can be read but that cannot be written into. This is the permanent portion of the computer memory.

Real Asset: See *fixed asset*.

Real Growth: Increase in supply or demand for goods or services associated with an increase in units or in the true value of units rather than simply an increase in unit price (inflation).

Real Time: Data management and manipulation at the same time that it is entered into the computer.

Reappointment Process: For members of a hospital medical staff, the credentialing and privileging steps that lead to renewed membership on the medical staff.

Reasonable and Customary Charge: The prevailing fee charged in a geographic area for a given procedure or treatment by physicians.

Reasonable Patient Standard: A physician is bound by duty to his patient to provide medical information that is pertinent to a patient's condition so that the patient can make a reasonable decision on treatment.

Reasonable Person Standard: A test often used by the fact finder (judge or jury) to measure conduct in his or her determination of negligence. The general level of care expected of individuals under the same or similar circumstances. For doctors defending themselves in a negligence suit, this generally refers to the behavior expected of a reasonable physician, familiar with the appropriate standards of practice that should be applied in circumstances such as those under question in the lawsuit.

Rebates: Refunds to consumers after a purchase.

Rebuttable Presumption: A legal presumption is a rule that allows the fact finder (judge or jury) to accept a fact as true if other underlying facts are proven. It is rebuttable when, depending on the jurisdiction, the party opposing the presumed fact is allowed to offer evidence to contradict it.

Recapitalization: See *reorganization*.

Receipt: A formal document that records the amount and nature of a transaction; in finance, monies received by cash, check, or by cash flow equivalent, regardless of the source of or the reason for the monies being received.

Receivable: An amount that an organization or individual is owed by another for goods or services supplied by the former to the latter.

Receivables Turnover: The length of time, on average, that is required to collect accounts receivable.

Receiver: The target of a message in the communication process, usually a potential customer.

Reciprocity: The trading of sales for sales.

Record: A grouping of data fields in a file that refers to information about a single entity.

Recredentialing Process: The steps used in determining whether a physician remains qualified to serve on a hospital's medical staff.

Reengineering: The search for and implementation of radical change in the processes of an organization in order to achieve breakthrough results.

Reenrollment: After an open enrollment period, the net number of subscribers in a managed care organization.

Reference Group: The people to whom an individual looks when forming attitudes about a particular topic.

Reference Price: The price a consumer expects to pay, or against which other alternatives are evaluated.

Referral: Provision of services by a provider not on an HMO's staff or not under contract.

Refunding: The issue of bonds to retire bonds currently outstanding.

Refusal: When a patient or a representative of the patient prevents or stops medical care. See *informed refusal*.

Register: A group of electronic switches in a computer that are used to store and manipulate data.

Registration Statement: Under federal law, a document that must be filed prior to the offering of securities for public sale.

Regression Analysis: A mathematical technique for determining the relationship among multiple attributes of observations (e.g., age, sex, diagnosis, frequency of visits to physicians) in a data set. Least-squares regression is a technique that determines the best linear relationships among the variables.

Regulation: A legally binding rule formulated by a government agency to implement legislation.

Reimbursement System: Any of several mechanisms—fee for service, Medicare prospective payment, etc.—by which providers and provider groups are paid for the delivery of health care services

Reinforcement: In the learning process, when the consumer's response is followed by satisfaction, that is, reduction in the drive.

Reinstatement: The process of restoring a lapsed policy.

Reinsurance: Insurance purchased by a health plan to protect it against excessive costs. The process by which an insurer transfers all or part of the insurance risk to another insurer.

Reinsurer: The insurance company that accepts the risk from another insurance company in a reinsurance transaction.

Relative Value Scale/Relative Value Unit: A set of index numbers associated with a collection of different activities (e.g., medical procedures) that provide an indication of differential value, physical inputs, cost, or any other attribute shared by the activities. Medicare payment to physicians is based on relative value units for about 7,000 procedures on separate scales for work, cost of practice, and malpractice expense, collectively called the *resource-based relative value scale (RBRVS)*.

Release: A mechanism by which an individual relinquishes his or her right to maintain a claim or cause of action.

Relevant Range: Activity levels above which fixed costs become variable.

Reminder Advertising: Advertising to keep the product's name before the public.

Renewal Premiums: Premiums payable after the first premium.

Renewal Provision: In an individual policy, the conditions under which the insurer may refuse to renew coverage, may cancel coverage, or may increase the premium.

Reorder Point: A predetermined point at which inventories are to be replenished, usually set so as to minimize the adverse effects of stock-outs.

Reorganization: A change in the capital structure of an organization that affects the rights and holdings of capital suppliers, especially equity suppliers.

Replacement Cost: The current market price for an asset.

Report Card: Tool used to compare and judge the performance of health care providers and health plans. See *Health Employer Data and Information Set*.

Repurchase Agreement: An arrangement under which a securities dealer agrees to repurchase a short-term security at a later date for a specified price plus interest; any such agreement relating to any asset.

Required Rate of Return: The minimum rate of return needed to attract capital infusions from each class of capital suppliers (e.g., debt, equity); the rate that adequately compensates a capital supplier for being deprived of the use of capital for some period and, during that period, bearing a variety of risks that the full value of the capital may not be recovered.

Requisition: A formal, written order for the use of assets, such as the withdrawal of supplies from inventory.

Reserves: Portion of premiums placed in a fund to cover unforeseen events.

Res Ipsa Loquitur: Literally, "the thing speaks for itself." A rule of evidence that allows a fact finder (judge or jury) to assume negligence when the instrument causing the injury was in the control of the defendant and when the incident does not ordinarily occur without negligence. For example, depending on the jurisdiction, pursuant to the doctrine of res ipsa loquitur, a jury may infer the existence of negligence on the part of a surgeon from the fact that a sponge was left in the patient; no other proof would be required. It is generally a rebuttable presumption that allows the defendant an opportunity to attempt to disprove his or her presumed negligence.

Research Proposal: A plan that specifies what marketing research information will be obtained and how.

Reserve for Bad Debts: See *allowance for bad debts*.

Reserves: Restricted cash investments or liquid investments to protect HMO enrollees against bankruptcy or insolvency.

Residual Value: The remaining value of a used asset; its value in liquidation. See *salvage value*.

Resolution: The amount of information that a video display can reproduce, expressed by the number of pixels in the display. High-resolution displays are smooth and realistic; low-resolution displays are jagged and blocky.

Resource Allocation: In an organization, the process of choosing which goods and services to produce and selecting the inputs that will best achieve the desired production.

Resource: Any input used in the production of goods or services.

Resource-Based Relative Value Scale (RBRVS): System used by HCFA to reimburse physicians on the basis of resources used for provision of care to Medicare patients. See *relative value scale*.

Respect and Caring: The degree to which patients are involved in care decisions and that those providing services do so with respect for patients' needs and expectations.

Respirator Brain: A pathological term used to describe the early stages of brain death.

Respondeat Superior: Literally, "let the master answer." A rule that holds a master liable for the acts of his or her servant, an employer for the acts of his or her employee, and a principal for the acts of his or her agent. It requires that the act for which the master, employer, or principal is held liable be done within the scope of the business. For example, a physician may be liable for the acts of his or her employed nurse in treating a patient.

Respondent: The party against whom an appeal is taken. More broadly, it often refers to any party that answers legal charges.

Response: An effort to satisfy a drive.

Response Rate: The percentage of people contacted in a research sample who complete the questionnaire.

Responsibility Accounting: Accounting that accumulates information from and reports information to organizational units responsible for producing revenue and/or incurring costs.

Responsive Pleading: A formal written answer to allegations set out in a pleading filed by another party.

Restraint of Trade: An agreement that restricts free and open competition.

Restricted Assets: Resources, the use of which is restricted by legal or contractual requirements, typically originating outside the organization. See *assets limited as to use*.

Restrictive Covenant: A portion of a contract that constrains the discretion of one of the parties; typically found in loan agreements and bond indentures limiting the financial degrees of freedom of the borrower.

Retailing: All of the activities involved in the sale of products to final consumers.

Retained Earnings: The historical accumulation of net income less the historical accumulation of dividends disbursed to equity suppliers.

Retrospective Payment: Determination of the payment amount for services after the services have been provided, typically based on the expense of providing those services. Examples include Medicare payments to so-called "TEFRA" (non-PPS) hospitals for inpatient services, payments to all hospitals for certain outpatient services, and payments by some Medicaid programs and some other third-party contracts.

Retrospective Reimbursement: Payment to providers on the basis of actual costs.

Retrospective Review: Computerized analysis of numerous claims to avoid the expense of case-by-case prior review. Used to establish utilization patterns.

Return of Capital: The repatriation of some or all of the value of an original capital infusion to the supplier of that capital.

Return of Debt: A principal payment.

Return of Equity: A liquidating dividend.

Return on Assets (ROA): A financial ratio given by organizational income for a given period divided by its total assets for that period.

Return on Capital: Any dollar or percentage return to a capital supplier over and above the return or preservation of the value of the original capital infusion.

Return on Debt: Interest.

Return on Equity: (1) In accounting, financial ratio given by organizational income for a given period divided by its total equity (accounting capital) for that period; (2) in finance, a dollar or percentage return to equity suppliers that may take the form of cash or in kind payments (dividends) and/or appreciation in the value of the equity claim.

Return on Investment (ROI): The ratio of net profit (after taxes) to the investment used to make the net profit. See *return on assets*; also used as a synonym for internal rate of return.

Returns to Capital: Any payment comprising a return of or a return on capital to capital suppliers.

Returns to Debt: Any principal or interest payments made to debt capital suppliers.

Returns to Equity: Any return of or on equity realized by the suppliers of that capital.

Revenue: The value, measured in monetary terms, received or expected to be received from the provision of goods and services.

Revenue Center: An area of business activity for which revenues are accumulated in accounting. Such centers are normally assigned both their own direct cost plus an allocation of costs from cost centers.

Reverse Channels: Channels used to retrieve products that customers no longer want.

Revolving Fund: Any account where funds are continually expended and replenished.

Revolving Line of Credit: A loan for which the outstanding principal is increased to meet the needs of the borrower and reduced when the borrower has cash in excess of needs.

Rider: An addition to an insurance policy that becomes part of the contract and limits or changes the benefits otherwise payable.

Rights: A privilege due one according to and conforming with morality, law, and justice.

Ring Network: A computer network in which individual units are connected in series, forming a continuous loop.

Risk: A measure of the variability of forecast amounts. The statistical probability of the occurrence of a loss or injury. Value varies inversely with risk. Risk sharing can be used as a utilization control mechanism in an HMO. In insurance, risk is defined as the probability of loss associated with a given population.

Risk-Adjusted Rate of Return: A discount rate for a stream of cash flows that is related to the level of risk in those cash flows.

Risk Adjustment: See *severity adjustment*.

Risk Analysis: A study of risks prior to entering a new venture. Used in strategy formulation.

Risk-Benefit Approach: A technique for judging the appropriateness of services in which the benefits to patients are balanced against the risks associated with the provision of the services. See *cost-benefit approach*.

Risk Bonus Arrangements: Incentive payment mechanism to share savings of delivering cost-efficient care.

Risk Class: A group of insureds who represent substantially similar risk to the insurer.

Risk Contract: A contract between an HMO or a CMP and HCFA to provide services to Medicare patients. The health plan gets a fixed monthly payment for enrolled Medicare patients and is obligated to provide all services for that payment.

Risk-Free Rate of Return: The required rate of return for suppliers of debt capital to the federal government; it is risk-free only in the sense that the risk of default in the payment of principal and interest is nearly zero.

Risk Management: A collection of techniques used by an organization to identify, evaluate, and reduce the potential for injuries to patients, staff, and visitors. Also refers to the activities undertaken by or on behalf of a defendant in a liability suit to reduce the risk of loss.

Risk Pool: Funds to be used to cover defined expenses. If not used at end of specified period, usually returned to managers of the risk.

Risk-Pooling: Spreading a portion of the risk to physicians.

Risk Premium: The difference between the risk-free rate of return and the required rate of return for a particular activity.

Risk Rating: The estimation of the likely health needs of a population and the variability in those needs, generally for the purpose of establishing insurance or HMO rates.

Risk Retention: The limitations on financial liability retained by an insurer or managed care organization.

Risk Sharing: Joint ownership by physicians and managed care organizations of the financial risk of providing services.

Risk-Taking: Formally bearing the uncertainties that are part of the marketing process.

Robinson-Patman Act: A 1936 federal law that makes illegal any price discrimination—e.g., selling the same products to different buyers at different prices—if it injures competition.

Rostral-Caudal ("head-to-tail"): A progression of signs and symptoms that indicate the extent of brain loss.

Routinized Response Behavior: The tendency of consumers to regularly select a particular way of satisfying a need when it occurs.

Rule for Maximizing Profit: The principal that a firm should produce that output where marginal cost is equal to but not greater than marginal revenue.

Run Chart: A simple graph used to depict changes in a process measurement over time. See *control chart*, in which control limits are added to the run chart.

RVS: See *relative value scale*.

S

S Corporation: A corporation that, under applicable tax regulations, is a pass-through entity. Its stockholders have limited liability for the debts of the corporation. See *C Corporation*.

Safe Harbor: A rule or regulation that carves out and makes legal an area of otherwise proscribed activity; those types of conduct that will not be considered to violate the general prohibition fall within the safe harbor. The term is commonly used to refer to descriptions of behavior that is legal under laws regulating medical business practices.

Safety: The degree to which risk in the health care environment for both patient and provider are reduced.

Sale and Lease-Back: A financial transaction in which the seller of an asset may subsequently use the asset under a lease.

Sale Price: A temporary discount from the list price.

Sales Analysis: A detailed breakdown of a company's sales records.

Sales Decline: A stage of the product life cycle when new products replace the old.

Sales Era: A time when a company emphasizes selling because of increased competition.

Sales Forecast: An estimate of the quantity of a product or service an industry or firm hopes to sell to a market segment.

Sales-Oriented Objective: Desire for some level of unit sales, dollar sales, or share of market, without reference to profit.

Sales Presentation: A salesperson's effort to make a sale.

Sales Promotion: Those promotion activities, other than advertising, publicity, and personal selling, that stimulate interest, trial, or purchase by final customers or others in the channel.

Salvage Value: The estimated or actual value of an asset when it is liquidated. See *residual value*.

Sample: A part of the relevant population in a research project.

Sampling Rate: The rate at which the value of an analog signal is measured and recorded.

Sanctity of Life: Considering life as sacred or holy.

Satisfaction: See *patient satisfaction*.

Saturation: Maximum penetration in a subscriber group or market by an HMO.

Scan: The process by which a picture, illustration, or document is examined to produce an image on a monitor screen or an image file in a computer.

Scanner: An optical device that recognizes a specified set of visual symbols.

Scarcity: A market condition in which demand for a good or service exceeds the supply.

Scatter Diagram: A chart on which data points representing a two-dimensional relationship between variables in a process are plotted so that general trends can be spotted.

Schedules: Lists of the specific amounts of money that the insurer will pay in benefits for specified treatments and procedures.

Schema: The overall organization of a database.

Science-Based Managed Care: Using evidence from patient outcomes to determine what techniques work and applying the techniques that work.

Scientific Method: A decision-making approach that focuses on being objective and orderly in testing ideas before accepting them.

Scrap Value: See *salvage value*.

Screen: The visual display portion of a computer monitor.

Screening: Methods used by managed care organizations to limit access to unnecessary care.

Scroll Bar: An element of a graphic user interface screen that allows the user to "scroll" down through a list of elements or down a page of data.

Second Insured Rider: A supplementary benefit rider that provides insurance coverage for another individual.

Second Opinion: Policy provision that requires an examination by a second physician before coverage for certain treatments or procedures is authorized by the insurer.

Secondary Care: Services provided by specialists to whom primary care physicians refer patients.

Secondary Data: Information derived through statistical or other mathematical manipulation of raw or primary data. For instance, medical record data (primary) can be used with financial data (primary) to develop physician profiles (secondary data).

Section 501(c)(3) Organization: A tax-exempt status under the Internal Revenue Code used for nonprofit organizations engaged in the provision of services in education, health care, or other specified "charitable" areas of activity.

Secured Claim: A claim for which collateral is pledged.

Securities and Exchange Commission (SEC): The federal agency that regulates the financial reporting activities and securities of publicly offered companies.

Securities: See *capital claim*.

Segmenters: Marketers who aim at one or more homogeneous segments and try to develop a different marketing mix for each segment.

Segmenting: An aggregating process that clusters people with similar needs into a market segment.

Selection Against the Insurer: See *adverse selection*.

Selection Grid: A method for selecting one of several option by ranking criteria and using those judged most important.

Selection of Risks: See *underwriting*.

Selective Contracting: Choosing a provider on the basis of successful outcomes for specific events.

Selective Demand: Demand for a company's own brand rather than a product category.

Selective Distribution: Selling through only those middlemen who will give the product special attention.

Selective Exposure: Tendency for people to seek out and notice only information that interests them.

Selective Perception: Tendency for people to screen out or modify ideas, messages, and information that conflict with previously accepted attitudes and beliefs.

Selective Retention: Tendency for people to remember only what they want to remember.

Self-Administered Group Insurance Plan: Policyholder performs most or all of the administrative aspects of the plan, calculating and sending the premium to the insurer on a regular basis.

Self-Funded Group: See *self-insured group*.

Self-Insured Group: A form of group insurance in which the group sponsor rather than an insurance company is financially responsible for claims. A group may be partially or fully self-insured.

Self-Insured Plan: A health plan in which an employer instead of the insurance company assumes the risk for medical cost.

Self-Referrals: Arrangements for specialty care made by the patient rather than the provider.

Selling Functions: Activities that promote a product or service.

Semantics: The relationship between the words and symbols in a computer program and the meaning assigned to them.

Semi-Fixed Costs: See *step costs*.

Semi-Variable Costs: See *step costs*.

Sensitivity Analysis: Varying the value of a parameter in a process to assess the parameter's impact on the outcome of the process. Sensitivity measures the probability that severity-adjusted outcomes will be poor, given substandard quality of care.

Sentinel Event Monitoring: Trending/evaluating adverse outcomes for patterns of poor care.

Sentinel Events: See *adverse events*.

Serial Bonds: Bonds the principal of which is divided into amounts that mature at different times throughout the life of the bond.

Server: A central device in a computer network that connects individual devices and users to the central processing unit for the network.

Service: A deed performed by one party for another.

Service Area: The geographic area in which an HMO provides service to members.

Service Industry: An organization or group of organizations whose business purpose is the provision of a service rather than the manufacture and sale of a product or good.

Service Life: The period of usefulness of an asset. See *economic life*.

Service Mark: Those words, symbols, or marks that are legally registered for use by a single company to refer to a service offering.

Service of Process: Delivery pursuant to the procedural rules of the jurisdiction of a document authorized by the law of the jurisdiction that commands the individual or entity to act or refrain from acting in a particular manner. For example, service of process accompanied by a complaint generally requires the individual named in the complaint to respond to the allegations within a set number of days.

Service Plan: An insurance plan that contracts directly with providers but not for managed care. Applies essentially only to Blue Cross and Blue Shield Plans.

Severity Adjustment: Use of any of a variety of mathematical and statistical techniques to make data on medical quality, resource utilization, outcomes, and adverse occurrences from different populations responsive to differing levels of seriousness in the diseases and injuries counted in the various populations' data.

Severity Measures: See *severity of illness indexes*.

Severity of Illness Indexes: Any of several proprietary systems for performing severity adjustments.

Severity Standardization: The principle that comparisons among providers and facilities can be made fairly only if severity is taken into account and if the severity adjustment techniques used are similar or the same.

Severity: A clinical characteristic of a patient related to the risk of mortality and morbidity that is predictive of treatment requirements. Severity is often measured in two different ways: On the basis of resource use (cost, length of stay) or on the basis of more clinical definitions (risk of death, treatment difficulty, clinical instability, extent of organ system involvement).

Shadow Pricing: Setting premium rates on the basis of those of a competitor. Generally considered unethical.

Shareholders: The owners of the stock in an organization. Sometimes referred to as stockholders, equity holders, or equity suppliers.

Sherman Act: Antitrust legislation passed in 1890 aimed at preserving free and unfettered competition. (15 U.S.C. 1-7). Section 1 prohibits contracts, combinations, and conspiracies that unreasonably restrain trade. Section 2 prohibits monopolization, attempts to monopolize, and conspiracies to monopolize.

Shewhart Cycle: See *plan-do-check-act cycle*.

Shoe Box Effect: Tendency of beneficiaries to save medical bills for group claim filing and then lose them, so that the insurer never pays.

Shopping Products: Products that a customer feels are worth the time and effort to compare with competing products.

Short-Term: In accounting, an adjective used to refer to liabilities or debt to be repaid at a time or times less than or equal to one year hence, and to assets expected to be used or maintained for periods of one year or less; more generally, referring to a limited, relatively brief period or to the time point at the end of such a period.

Simple Trade Era: A time when families traded or sold their surplus output to local middlemen who resold these goods to other consumers or distant middlemen.

Simulation: Comparison of operating statements with and without a payer contract. It also shows variations in rate structures, activity levels and more.

Single Target Market Approach: Process of segmenting the market and picking one of the homogeneous segments as the firm's target market.

Single-Payer System: Assumption of funding responsibility by government or another entity. Also, assumption by multiple payers of single set of payment standards.

Single-Service Plan: A health plan that offers specialized health care, e.g., podiatry, mental health, or chiropractic.

Sinking Fund: An account consisting of assets and their earnings that are restricted for use in retiring bonds or other long-term obligations.

Situational Analysis: An informal study of information already available in the problem area.

Skilled Labor: Employees or groups of employees who function in a specialist role within an organization.

Skilled Nursing Facility (SNF): High-level specialized care used as an alternative to extended hospitalization or intense home care.

Skimming Price Policy: Practice of trying to sell the top of the market—the top of the demand curve—at a high price before aiming at more price-sensitive customers.

Slippery Slope Arguments: Used in a court of law as expressions of the principle of nonmaleficence, specifically the consideration of whether harm may have resulted from innocent intentions. See *wedge arguments*.

Small Subscriber Group Aggregate: Small businesses, professional associations, or other groups established as a subscriber group.

Small-Area Analysis: A statistical technique that involves the collection and evaluation of data on a given subject in a narrow geographic area for comparison with similar data collected in other areas. In health care quality determinations, usually used to compare the incidence of procedure or treatment patterns for physicians.

Smart Card: Under managed competition, each American would carry a plastic identification card that would allow them to access medical services included in the basic benefit package.

SMSA: Standard metropolitan statistical area.

SOAP: Subjective, objective, assessment, and plan.

SOAPIE: Subjective, objective, assessment, plan, implementation, and evaluation.

Social Conscience: See *morals*.

Social Cost of Capital: A discount rate used to evaluate societal investments and programs.

Social HMO (SHMO): A demonstration project to integrate acute and long-term care for Medicare beneficiaries.

Social Imperative: An obligation of benefit to society.

Social Insurance Supplement Policy: A medical expense policy that provides benefits complementary to those form a specified government insurance program.

Social Needs: Needs concerned with love, friendship, status, and esteem, things that involve a person's interaction with others.

Social Quality: In health care, the equitable distribution of health care services among a population.

Social Responsibility: A firm's obligation to improve its positive effects on society and reduce its negative effects.

Software: The programs or instructions that instruct a computer. Software may be built into the computer's ROM or loaded as needed from disk or tape.

Sole Shareholder Professional Corporation: An IPA that is privately held by one owner.

SOP: Standard operating procedure.

Sorting: Process of separating products into grades and qualities desired by different target markets.

Soundex: A search mechanism that permits looking up a "text" name by selecting the first few consonants of text to find potential homonyms and misspellings.

Source: The sender of a message.

Sources and Uses Statement: See *statement of cash flows*.

Spatial Resolution: A measure of the ability to distinguish on a monitor screen between proximate points.

Special Damages: See *conceptual damages*.

Specialty HMO: HMO organized to provide services in a specific specialty area.

Specialty Products: Consumer products that the customer really wants and makes a special effort to find.

Specificity Analysis: Varying the value of a parameter in a process to assess the parameter's impact on the outcome of the process. Specificity measures the probability that severity-adjusted outcomes will be good, given good quality of care.

Spend-Down Case: A patient who is medically needy or has catastrophic medical expenses.

Sperm Banking: Storing sperm for future use to produce a child.

Spin-Off: A new organization that is created from activities of a parent or existing organization.

Spreadsheet: A software program that organizes data and formulas into a matrix of cells.

Staff Model: One HMO model in which the assumption of risk and the provision of care are in a single legal entity, typically owning physical facilities and employing salaried medical professionals, including physicians. A form of closed-panel HMO.

Standard: A value or criterion established by authority, custom, or general consent as a model or example to guide performance and to measure quantity or quality.

Standard Cost: An expected or target cost, estimated in advance by management on the basis of forecasts of quantities and prices of input resources.

Standard Industrial Classification (SIC) Codes: Codes used to identify groups of firms in similar lines of business.

Standardization and Grading: Process of sorting products according to size and quality.

Standard of Care: Community-based guidelines for provision of health care services for a given diagnosis. The level of conduct against which one's acts are measured to determine liability.

Standard Premium Rate: The rate charged for a person classified as having an average or less than average probability of loss.

Standard Risk: A person possessing an average or less-than-average likelihood of loss.

Standing: The legal capacity to sue for relief.

Staples: Products that are bought often, routinely, and without much thought.

Star Network: A computer network configuration in which individual work-stations are arranged in parallel.

Stare Decisis: "Let the decision stand"; the legal doctrine that prescribes adherence to those precedents set forth in cases that have been decided.

State Board of Licensure: State-level agency that regulates entry to practice for professionals. May also regulate the scope of activities of health care organizations.

State Data Commissions: Agencies established under the Health Care Quality Improvement Act of 1986 to collect information for submission to the National Practitioner Data Bank.

Statement of Cash Flows: A financial accounting statement for a given period that reconciles amounts reported on the income statement for that same period and changes between the balance sheets at the beginning and end of that period, all tied to reconcile with changes between beginning and ending cash balances; in essence a misnomer, in that the statement neither measures nor describes actual cash flows.

Statement of Financial Position: See *balance sheet*.

Statement of Revenues and Expenses: See *income statement*.

Static Budget: See *fixed budget*.

Statistical Process Control: The use of statistics to monitor and control the quality of manufacturing processes.

Status Quo Objectives: Objectives that support the current posture and operations of an organization.

Statute of Frauds: The legal requirement that certain contracts must be made in writing and cannot be enforced if they are only oral agreements.

Statute of Limitations: The time within which a claim must be brought. The period is generally established by statute and varies according to the type of claim at issue. For example, the statute of limitations might be different for professional malpractice as opposed to other types of negligence actions.

Statutory Law: Law created by state and federal legislative bodies.

Statutory Merger: The acquisition of 51 or more percent of a corporation's stock, such that the purchased organization ceases to exist as a separate entity.

Step Costs: Cost behavior that, over a relevant range of volume, combines elements of both fixed and variable costs.

Stipulation: An agreement by attorneys on opposite sides of a case as to any matter pertaining to the proceedings.

Stock-Out: The depletion of the inventory of an asset.

Stop-Loss Protection: A form of insurance that offers protection for medical costs above a specified limit on an annual basis.

Stop-Loss Provision: Specification that the insurer will pay all of an insured's medical expenses after a specified amount of out-of-pocket expenses. An element of the coinsurance provision.

Storage: A device or medium that can accept, hold, and deliver data on demand.

Storing: The marketing function of holding goods.

Storyboards: Poster displays that depict a quality improvement process, usually in graphic form.

Straight Rebuy: A routine repurchase that may have been made many times before.

Strategic (Management) Planning: The managerial process of developing and maintaining a match between an organization's resources and its market opportunities.

Strategic Partners (Strategic Alliances): Joint ventures, license agreements, comarketing arrangements, or subcontracting that complement the organization and enhance its market position.

Strike Price: The price at which an option (put or call) can be exercised.

Structured Query Language (SQL): A standardized language used for querying, updating, and managing relational databases.

Structured Settlement: A method of paying an agreed upon amount that generally allows predetermined payments to be made periodically.

Subcontracting: A form of strategic alliance in which some services are farmed out.

Subdirectory: A collection of files packaged in a directory that is contained within a larger directory of files and other subdirectories.

Subjective Component: Condition perceived by the patient and not the examiner.

Subordinated Debenture: A debt security that receives principal and interest payments only if there is money available after obligations to more senior capital claims have been met.

Suborn: A term in criminal law indicating the procurement of another to commit perjury.

Subpoena: A judicially enforceable order to present oneself at a time and place, generally to testify or produce and authenticate documents or other items.

Subrogation: The right of a health plan to recover money paid to a member after that member receives payments as a result of legal action.

Subscriber: An employer, association, or other group that contracts with an HMO for a prepaid health care plan.

Substandard Premium Rate: A higher premium rate charged for insurance for the person with greater-than-average likelihood of loss.

Substandard Risk: A person possessing a greater-than-average likelihood of loss.

Substantive Due Process: In general, those rights that spring from U.S. Constitution guarantees, found in the 5th and 14th Amendments, that no person may be deprived of life, liberty, or property without due process of law. It is distinguishable from procedural due process, which guarantees a fair method for determining whether one's substantive rights have been violated. See *due process*.

Substituted Judgment: A premise that holds that patients should have the right to make treatment decisions by virtue of their autonomy and privacy regardless of whether they are deemed competent.

Substitutes: Products that offer the buyer a choice.

Summary Judgment: A procedure whereby either party may, if there are no controverted issues of fact, submit a matter to a judge alone for his or her determination. In essence, the party is asking the judge to apply the law to the facts and render a judgment. It may be sought as to the entire or any part of the dispute. For example, a court may determine by summary judgment that one side is liable to the other, but leave the issue of damages for the later trial. Summary judgment is difficult to obtain in negligence actions.

Summons: A form of process, often served with the complaint, commencing an action. It directs the individual upon whom it is served to act (e.g., answer the complaint) within the time set out therein.

Sunk Costs: Past outlays, the amounts of which are nonrecoverable, regardless of whether they have been recognized by accounting as expenses.

Supererogatory Actions: Exceeding a moral obligation; doing more than promised or necessary.

Superimposed Major Medical Insurance: See *supplemental major medical coverage*.

Superstandard Risk: See *preferred risk*.

Supplemental Health Services: Benefits offered by an HMO that exceed its basic health service requirements as defined by federal regulations.

Supplemental Insurance: See *wraparound plan*.

Supplemental Major Medical Coverage: A major medical policy issued in conjunction with a hospital-surgical expense policy.

Supplies: Expense items that do not become a part of a finished product.

Supply: The quantity of a good or service that a producer or provider is willing to place in the market at a given price.

Supply Curve: A graphical depiction of the quantity of products that will be supplied at various possible prices.

Supply-Driven System: Provision of services dictated and priced by organization delivering care.

Surgery Package Fees: A major reimbursement method for surgical procedures. The fees include the preoperative evaluation, all hospital visits, and a certain time as an outpatient following surgery. See *global fee*.

Surgical Case Review: A technique for studying the appropriateness and effectiveness of surgical procedures in a health care organization.

Surgical Schedule: A specification in a policy of the maximum payment benefits for named surgical procedures.

Surgicenter: See *freestanding outpatient surgical center*.

Surrogate: Person legally appointed to represent and carry out the interests and wishes of an individual in the provision of medical care.

Surveillance: Systematic review of patients' medical records to detect and flag conditions that merit attention.

Sutton's Law: "Go where the money is!" A remark credited to Depression-era bank robber Willy Sutton. Although Sutton denies having said it, the phrase is still used to sum up what needs attention in a managed care plan.

Syntax: The rules that govern the structure of a computer language and its expressions. The computer issues an error message when language syntax is violated.

System: Any group of related processes intended to achieve a specific outcome.

System Program: Software program that governs the internal operations of the computer. See *application program*.

Systems Theory: Principles, models, and laws that apply to complex interrelationships and interdependencies of sets of linked components that form a functioning whole and that themselves may be systems.

Tab: A carriage control that specifies output columns.

Taft-Hartley Groups: Unions and other multiple-employer groups targeted by the Taft-Hartley Act. Also the bargaining units that allowed under the act. The National Labor Relations Board allows up to eight bargaining units for hospital workers, taken from four groups—RNs, all other professionals, service and maintenance employees, and technical employees.

TAG: Technical advisory group.

Takeover: The actual or intended acquisition of one organization by another.

Tangible Asset: See *fixed asset*.

Target Market: A fairly homogeneous group of customers to whom a company wishes to appeal. The population a managed care company wants to capture.

Target Marketing: Tailoring of the marketing mix to fit some specific target customers.

Target Market Potential: The quantity of a product or service that a whole market segment might buy.

Target Return Objective: The establishment of a specific level of profit as an objective.

Target Return Pricing: Establishing prices to cover all costs and achieve a target return.

Task List: A list of things to be done or items to be obtained.

Task Method: An approach to development of a budget that bases the budget on the job to be done.

Task Utility: Value provided when someone performs a task for someone else, for instance when a bank handles financial transactions.

Tax Basis: The cost of an asset adjusted for improvements and for depreciation and other cost recoveries, used for calculation of taxable gains and losses when the asset is liquidated.

Tax Credit: An amount that is subtracted from taxes otherwise due.

Tax Equity and Fiscal Responsibility Act of 1982 (TEFRA): The original attempt to bring prospective payment to inpatient services under Medicare, this law was largely superseded by the DRG legislation in 1983. The law continues to govern financial arrangements for institutions and organizations not covered by the DRG prospective payment system. Includes provisions governing the payment by Medicare for certain specialty inpatient hospitalizations, including rehabilitation, psychiatric, cancer, long-term acute care, and care provided by children's hospitals.

Tax Exemption: Provisions in tax law or regulation that define the conditions under which an individual or organization may forgo payment of various taxes, especially income tax but also, commonly, property (ad valorem) taxes, excise or sales taxes, and taxes on intangibles.

Tax Expenditure: The reduction in taxes received by a taxation authority related to a tax credit, tax exemption, or tax shield.

Tax Liability: The amount of taxes expected to be owed or owed by an entity to a government agency.

Tax Preference: A deduction or credit that, if it exceeds specified amounts, may expose the taxpayer to the alternative minimum tax.

Tax Shield: An expense, such as depreciation, that decreases taxable income without a concomitant disbursement.

Technological Imperative: An obligation to apply technology to the body of scientific knowledge wherever possible.

Technology Assessment: The systematic and scientific evaluation of the cost- and risk-effectiveness of both existing and new forms of technology.

TEFRA: See *Tax Equity and Fiscal Responsibility Act.*

Telemarketing: Use of the telephone to call on customers or prospects.

Telemedicine: The provision of medical diagnosis and consulting services by long-distance electronic means.

Teleological Theories: Theories that focus on consequences. In unclear situations, teleological theories are based on choosing the best alternative.

Telephone and Direct Mail Retailing: Marketing technique that allows consumers to shop at home, usually placing orders by mail or by a toll-free telephone call and charging purchases to credit cards.

Temporal Resolution: The amount of time between acquisition by the computer of each of a series of images.

Temporary Insurance Agreement: Specified period of coverage between first premium payment and application for insurance and acceptance of the policy by the insurer.

Temporary Restraining Order (TRO): A court order to do or refrain from doing some act that is of a very limited duration and is intended to maintain the status quo while additional information and evidence are gathered.

Ten-Step Procedure: The continuous quality improvement process formulated by the Joint Commission on Accreditation of Healthcare Organizations as a part of its Agenda for Change accreditation program for hospitals. An expansion of JCAHO five-stage approach to quality improvement, the 10-step procedure involves identification of responsibility, scope, and priorities; verification of indicators, thresholds, and analysis; the plan; action; and evaluation and communication.

Term Loan: A loan with a specified maturity date.

Terminable at Will: A contract that can terminated at any time without cause is said to be terminable at will.

Terminal: The collection of devices used to input data and programs to the computer and to receive output from the computer.

Termination: Removal or discontinuation of medical care, whether by refusal of treatment by the patient, by a physician's decision, or by a determination of death.

Tertiary Care: Health care services provided by highly specialized medical centers, usually highly technological in nature.

Text Editor: A software program for the preparation and manipulation of written material.

Text Scanner: A device for the translation of printed documents into computer language.

Thanatology: The study of death as it relates to the patient and his or her family.

Therapeutic Abortion: Ending the life of a fetus to save the life of the mother.

Therapeutic Genetics: Insertion of a specific gene replacement into fertilized eggs, fetuses, or individuals to correct a genetic disorder.

Therapeutic Privilege: An exception to the rule that an informed consent must be obtained prior to therapy. It generally requires that the disclosure of information would likely worsen the patient's condition or render him or her so emotionally distraught as to hinder effective therapy. It is not an excuse to omit disclosure because of the physician's concern that a competent patient will elect to forgo the care.

Third-Generation Managed Care: Form of managed care being shaped by employer demands for cost control and provider efforts to manage reimbursement.

Third-Party Administrator: An organization that administers insurance benefits for a self-insured group but that accepts no responsibility for the funds that pay claims. See *administrative services only (ASO) contract* and *self-insured group*.

Third-Party Payer: Public or private entity that pays for the provision of health care to employees on behalf of employers.

Third-Party Policy: A policy owned by a person other than the insured.

Three-Tier Rate: Structure that sets monthly premiums on the basis of single-person, two-person, and family coverage.

Timeliness: The degree to which care is provided to patients at the most beneficial time or at the time of greatest need.

Time-Share Mode: Simultaneous operation of a computer by several users. Because of the speed of computers, what is actually sequential access appears to be simultaneous.

Times Interest Earned: An indication of the ability of an organization to meet obligations to debt suppliers, calculated as the ratio given by pretax income and interest expense divided by interest expense.

Time Utility: The value of having a product available when the customer wants it.

Tort: A private or civil (not criminal) wrong or injury as a result of a legal duty that exists because of society's expectations regarding interpersonal conduct (as opposed to an expectation created by contract). Torts generally involve personal injuries.

Tortfeasor: A person or entity who has committed a civil wrong, other than breach of contract, resulting in loss or injury for which there is a judicial remedy.

Total Cost: The sum of total fixed and total variable costs.

Total Fixed Cost: The sum of those costs that are fixed in total, no matter how much is produced.

Total Quality Management (TQM): A management system for continuously improving the quality of an organization's products or services that is directed from the top management levels and involves all employees in improvement of processes rather than the performance of individuals.

Total Return Concept: The inclusion of interest, dividends, and capital appreciation in the determination of income.

Total Variable Cost: The sum of those changing expenses that are closely related to output, such as expenses for parts, wages, packaging materials, outgoing freight, and sales commissions.

Touch Screen: A monitor screen on which commands can be entered by pressing designated areas with a finger or other object.

Town and Gown: Expression used to encompass the frequently ragged relationships between physicians in an academic health center and those in the surrounding community.

TQM: Total quality management.

Traceability: In cost accounting, the ability to assign a cost to a cost object.

Tracer Diagnoses: Sample conditions used for evaluating provider care.

Trade Credit: Debt arising from the exchange of resources, goods or services in the marketplace. See *accounts receivable*, *accounts payable*, *payable*, and *receivable*.

Trademark: Those words, symbols, or marks that are legally registered for use by a single company.

Trade-Off Analysis: See *conjoint analysis*.

Traditional Channel System: A channel in which the various channel members make little or no effort to cooperate with each other.

Transaction: An event that triggers the recognition, recording, or posting of a numerical depiction (usually in monetary terms) of the event. For private-sector organizations, a typical transaction in accounting is the actual delivery of a good or service to a patient or the creation/elimination of a claim by or on the organization; in finance, it is the actual receipt or disbursement of money or a cash flow equivalent.

Treasury Bill: A short-term discounted debt security issued by the U.S. government in maturities of up to one year.

Treasury Bond: An interest-bearing debt security issued by the U.S. government in maturities of up to 30 years.

Treasury Note: An interest-bearing debt security issued by the U.S. government in maturities of up to 10 years.

Trend Extension: Use of past experience to predict the future.

Trending: Calculation of potential future utilization on the basis of past utilization.

Triage: Evaluation of patients' condition on the basis of urgency and seriousness of need for treatment.

Trial Court: The court in which the evidence is presented to either a judge or a jury for decision.

Triple Option: The offering of an HMO, a PPO, and an indemnity plan by a single carrier to a single group of insureds.

Turfing: Culling out of sick patients by physicians to improve their utilization profiles.

Turnkey: A prepackaged computer system containing all the hardware, software, training, and maintenance needed for a given application.

Turnover: The number of times during a given period that the value of one item (e.g., assets) is represented by another item (e.g., revenue).

Two-Tier Rate: Structure that sets monthly premiums on the basis of single-person and family coverage.

Tying arrangement: An arrangement where one party sells a product or service (the tying product) only on the condition that the buyer also purchase a different (or tied) product or service.

U

UBS: See *Uniform Billing Form*.

UHDDS: See *Uniform Hospital Discharge Data Set*.

Ultra Vires: Actions by a corporation that violate its charter.

Unbundling: Billing for individual components of a treatment that were previously billed as a unit.

Undersecured Claim: A secured claim in which the value of the collateral is less than the value of the claim.

Underutilization: The provision of less care in the diagnosis and treatment of patients than would be indicated by practice norms. In global terms, lack of access to health care services on the parts of selected components of the population.

Underwriters: Insurance professionals who are responsible for evaluating and classifying the degree of risk represented by proposed insureds.

Underwriting: Analysis of a group to determine rates or whether coverage should be offered. Also, health screening of each insurance applicant and refusing to cover preexisting conditions. The purchase of an entire securities offering by a single buyer or a small group of buyers, usually for resale, thereby guaranteeing, for a fee, that the offerer receives a set amount of money at a set time for the securities.

Undesired Markets: Situation that occurs whenever either the quantity or the quality of exchange transactions between the organization and its constituents differs from the desired.

Unfair Trade Practice Acts: Various laws that set a lower limit on prices, especially at the wholesale and retail levels.

Uniform Anatomical Gift Act: A statute adopted by every state that makes it legally possible for individuals to make known their intentions, while living, to donate their organs after death.

Uniform Billing Form (UBS): The form required for submission of secondary data for billing purposes in the Medicare program.

Uniform Determination of Death Act: A law that defines death as "irreversible cessation of all functions of the entire brain, including the brain stem." The most recent definition is "irreversible cessation of circulatory and respiratory function; or irreversible cessation of all functions of the entire brain, including the brain stem."

Uniform Hospital Discharge Data Set (UHDDS): The form required for abstracting medical information from the medical record for submission to Medicare in the billing process.

Unincorporated Association: A legal form of organization that is achieved by merely adopting a set of articles and bylaws.

Unit Pricing: Practice of placing the price per ounce (or some other standard measure) on or near the product.

United States Per Capita Costs (USPCC): The prospective national average per capita cost to the Medicare program per Medicare enrollee.

Universal Product Code (UPC): Special identifying marks (bar code) for each product readable by electronic scanners.

Universalizability: Able to be extended to everyone.

UNIX: A powerful computer operating system with many high-level utility programs that is capable of running a number of jobs simultaneously.

Unnecessary Procedure: A procedure that will not improve the condition of the patient.

Unproved Procedure: See *experimental procedure*.

Unrealized Gain (Loss): A gain (loss) in value that has not yet been realized through conversion to cash, to another asset, or by the reduction in a capital claim.

Unrealized Market: A group of potential buyers for which the desired transactions aren't taking place.

Unrelated Business Income: Any income that is not generated by activities directly related to the main purpose of the organization. Such income is fully taxable, regardless of the tax status of the organization.

Unsecured Claim: A claim that is not secured by any collateral.

Unsought Products: Products that potential customers don't yet want or know they can buy.

Upcoding: Billing for a procedure that is worth more money than the actual service performed.

Upload: To transfer user data to a remote computer system. To transfer data from a disk or other storage device to a computer.

Urgent Care Center: Medical facility for treatment of walk-in nonemergency ambulatory patients.

Usual, Customary, and Reasonable (UCR): A method for basing reimbursement for provider services on a profile of prevailing rates in a community.

Utilitarianism: A common form of consequentialism. Also a type of cost-benefit analysis in which ethical and other costs are weighed against the benefits of all alternatives.

Utility: The power to satisfy human needs. In decision analysis, a value a person places on an event or outcome.

Utilization: Patterns of use of resources or of provision of services over time. The ratio given by the amount of a resource used divided by the amount available for use. Utilization experience multiplied by the average cost per unit of service delivered equals capitated costs.

Utilization Control: Any methodology for controlling the use of resources.

Utilization Data: Information collected on physician practice patterns.

Utilization Management (UM): Any overall organizational strategy an methodology for ensuring that services are provided in the most effective and efficient manner and in conformance with established criteria.

Utilization Review (UR): A key element in utilization management activities, UR is a systematic assessment of medical records and other documentation to meet the goals of utilization management.

Utilization Standards: Average utilization criteria established on the basis of physician practice patterns.

V

Vacate: Where a court sets aside a previously entered order or decision; to render void.

Validation Criterion: Determination of whether diagnosis or problem was ascribed to patient in medical record.

Validity: The extent to which data measures what it is intended to measure.

Value: The desirability of products and services as evidenced by exchanges by an organization and its constituencies.

Value Added: The value of a good or service minus the cost of the resources used to produce or provide it.

Value Creation: See *net present value*.

Value Pricing: The practice of setting a fair price level for a marketing mix that gives customers what they need.

Value Purchasing: See *prudent buyer*.

Value Statements: A formal declaration denoting a principle, a standard, or a quality regarded as worthwhile or desirable.

Values: Standards held by individuals or set by groups of individuals or society.

Variable Budget: See *flexible budget*.

Variable Costs: Costs that change with activity levels; in particular, the costs of resources that are consumed if and only if an activity level is actually achieved.

Variable Memory: See *random-access memory (RAM)*.

Variance: The difference between a projected or a standard figure and the actual figure; types of variances include cost variances, revenue variances, price or rate variances, and quantity variances.

Variance Analysis: Study of the causes of differences between planned or anticipated amounts and actual amounts.

Variance Days: Nonacute days spent in hospitals.

Variance Management: The establishment of thresholds and focusing of attention on outcomes that fail to meet them.

Variation Analysis: Statistical techniques for measuring nature and the extent of deviations from accepted norms of performance.

Venue: The locale in which a court with authority over the persons and subject matter may hear cases. It is the geographical area within which an action may be brought.

Verdict: The final decision of the judge or jury on the matter presented for consideration.

Vertical Integration: The coordination of services among operating units that are at different stages of the process of delivery of patient services. Examples include a system's ownership or affiliation with home health agencies, hospices, single and multispecialty group practices, and rehabilitation services in addition to acute inpatient care. Vertical integration may be further distinguished by its direction: forward toward the customer, as in linkages with physician group practices, or backward toward suppliers, as in the case of owning a medical supply and equipment company.

Vertical Marketing Systems: Channel systems in which the whole channel focuses on the same target market at the end of the channel.

VGA (Video Graphics Array): Standard PC display standard that provides medium resolution for text and graphics.

Vicarious Liability: Often referred to as passive or secondary negligence, this term refers to the responsibility for injury or loss imposed on one party for the acts of another with whom he or she has a requisite relationship. For example, an employer is vicariously liable for the negligent acts of an employee committed in the course of employment.

Video Display Terminal: A monitor and keyboard for computer input and output.

Virtual Memory: The use of auxiliary data storage units as if they were computer memory.

Vital Few and Trivial Many Concept: The tendency in any group of a small number of people to skew a factor that is being measured.

Voice Recognition: Direct conversion of spoken data into computer language.

Voir Dire: Literally, "to speak the truth." This is the procedure whereby prospective jurors are questioned prior to determining who will sit in judgment on a case. Depending on the court, the questioning may be conducted by either the judge, counsel for the parties, or both.

Voluntary Termination Rate: See *lapse rate*.

Voluntary Trade Association: A private-sector organization representing the interests of a specified group of organizations or individuals for lobbying purposes.

Voucher: A document that recognizes a liability and authorizes disbursement of money, goods, or services to cover it.

Voucher System: In Medicare, a system in which beneficiaries would select from competing private plans and pay the difference between the Medicare voucher and the remainder of the premium.

Voxel: The smallest unit of a three-dimensional computer image. See *pixel*.

Waiting Period: See *probationary period.*

Wants: Needs that are learned during a person's life.

Warranty: The conditions and characteristics that the seller promises to deliver with regard to its product or service.

Wedge Arguments: See *slippery slope arguments.*

Weighted Average Required Rate of Return: The average required rate of return for an organization determined by weighting the required rate of return for each class of capital by the proportion of the total market value of the organization that class of capital represents, and summing the results over all classes of capital.

Weighted-Average Cost of Capital: The average cost of capital for an organization determined by weighting the cost of each class of capital by the proportion of the total market value of the organization that class of capital represents, and summing the results over all classes of capital.

Wheel of Retailing Theory: The principle that new types of retailers enter the market as low-status, low-margin, low-price operators and, if they are successful, evolve into high-margin, high-status operators, allowing room for new low-margin, low-status entries.

Whipsawing: A frowned-upon tactic used by some managed care companies whereby hospitals and physicians are pitted against each other in an attempt to force participation. Sometimes, after key physicians have been lured from hospital medical staffs, the hospital is forced to participate at a lower rate of reimbursement.

Wholesalers: Firms whose main function is providing marketing activities at earlier stages of the distribution channel.

Wholly Owned Subsidiary: A firm operated separately but owned by a parent company.

Wide-Area Network: A network that connects computers dispersed over a large geographic area.

Wild Card: A computer technique that allows performance of utility functions on multiple files with similar names. Commonly involves the use of an asterisk or some other code as the wild card designation.

Windows®: A powerful operating system that allows monitor display of two or more programs simultaneously.

Wire transfer: A method, using the facilities of the Federal Reserve System, for moving money from one institution to another. Generally, an electronic method for moving money from one organization or entity to another.

Withdrawal Rate: See *lapse rate*.

Withhold: The percentage of payment a managed care provider receives as a result of a contract with a managed care organization. It is common practice to return some or all of the withhold, depending on the total cost of referrals or hospital services and to the HMO and the relationship of the total cost to its budget.

Withholding: Intentional refusal or denial of medical care.

Word Processing: Any of several software programs for writing, revising, manipulating, formatting, and printing text for letters, reports, manuscripts, and other printed matter.

Word Wrapping: A word processing technique that automatically moves a word to the next line if it doesn't fit at the end of the original line.

Word: A sequence of bits that are accessed in memory as a unit.

Workers' Compensation: Government-mandated insurance that provides benefits to employees and their dependents in the event of an employee's job-related injury, disease, or death.

Working Capital: Current assets. See *net working capital*.

Workstation: A configuration of computer equipment and peripheral devices that are intended for use by a single person.

Work-Up: The record of the total evaluation for a patient.

WORM (Write Once Read Many): A technology for recording data on optical media in such a way that they cannot be edited, or overwritten but can be read multiple times.

Wraparound Plan: Insurance or health plan coverage for costs not covered by base plan.

Writ of Certiorari: An order issued by an appeals court upon the application of either party. It is used when the parties do not have an automatic right to have the matter considered by the appellate court but, rather, where the appeals court has discretion to hear the matter if it so elects. If granted, it is an order to the lower court in which the matter is pending to forward the record to the appellate court for its consideration.

Wrongful Death: A cause of action for the recovery of losses occasioned by the death of an individual caused by civil wrong. Wrongful death actions are ordinarily governed by state statutes.

WYSIWYG (What You See Is What You Get): In word processing programs, screen images—typefaces, format, etc.—that appear exactly as they will in the printed document.

Y

Yield: A variation on the internal rate of return for a set of cash flows; generally used in conjunction with bonds.

Z

Zero Defects: In quality measurement, the goal of perfection in the manufacture of products or provision of services.

Zero-Base Budgeting: Approach to budgeting for a given period in which all budget accounts are reduced to zero and are rebuilt on the basis of anticipated rather than historical activities.

Zone Pricing: The practice of using an average freight charge for shipments to all buyers within specific geographic areas.

Zygote Banking: Storing a cell formed by the union of a man and woman for future use in producing a child.

DATE DUE

GAYLORD

PRINTED IN U.S.A.